AMERICAN MISSIONARIES AMONG THE BULGARIANS: (1858-1912)

Tatyana Nestorova

EAST EUROPEAN MONOGRAPHS, BOULDER
DISTRIBUTED BY COLUMBIA UNIVERSITY PRESS, NEW YORK

1987

EAST EUROPEAN MONOGRAPHS, NO. CCXVIII

ISBN 0-88033-114-3
Library of Congress Catalog Card Number 87-80386

Printed in the United States of America

To My Father

TABLE OF CONTENTS

LIST OF TABLES AND ILLUSTRATIONS

MISSIONARY STATIONS OF THE AMERICAN BOARD AMONG THE BULGARIANS: 1858–1912

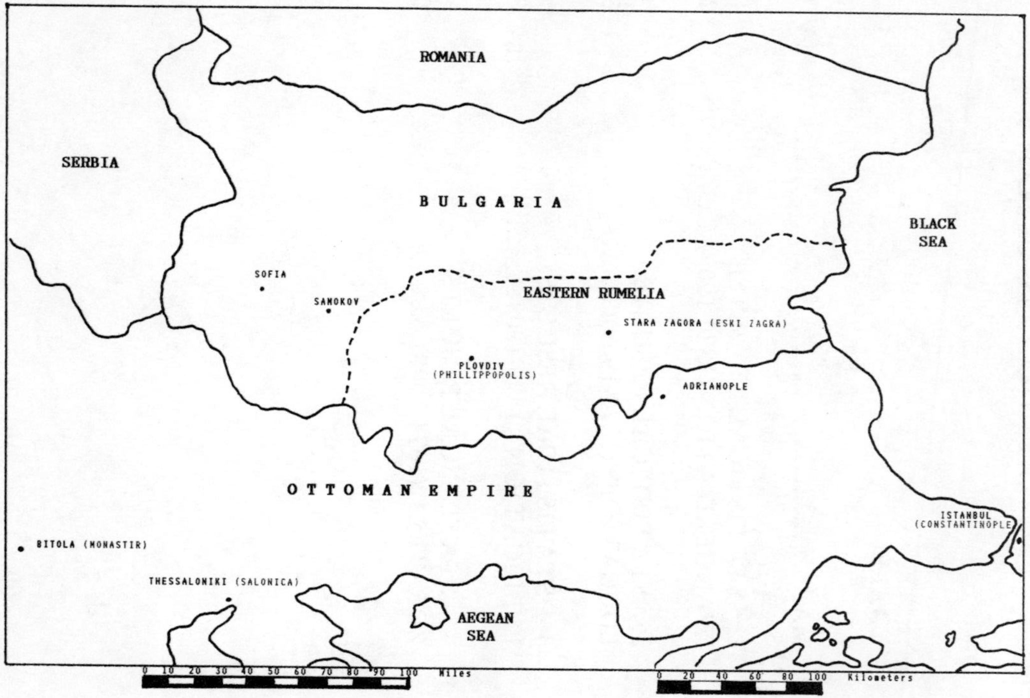

INTRODUCTION

Modern Balkan history is rich in examples of outside influences and foreign penetrations by various forces, trends and movements. One such episode is the history of American missionary involvement among the Bulgarian population in the region. The second half of the nineteenth century became the backdrop for the establishment of that special Bulgarian mission of the American Board of Commissioners for Foreign Missions (hereafter, the American Board).

The purpose of this study is to investigate the mission to determine the effects of the conscious missionary effort to change the religious outlook of an entire people. The problem is approached from several perspectives, the most important of which are discussions of different areas of American involvement and an evaluation of the missionary and native perceptions of each other and of the goals and accomplishments of the organization in Bulgaria. The method of presentation is topical-chronological: each major sphere of missionary activity is studied separately but in a chronological manner wherever possible. In addition, an attempt is made to assemble all statistical data related to the work of the American Board in order to supply a more accurate and complete picture of the missionary effort.

The study is chronologically limited to a period of fifty-four to fifty-five years. The starting point is roughly the beginning of the Bulgarian mission of the American Board in 1858. Its work is traced to the time of the Balkan Wars, 1912-1913, which was chosen as the closing date because of the impact of the Wars on Bulgarian history. The Wars initiated a period of substantial and irreversible setbacks in the Bulgarian attempt to solve the problem of national unification. In addition to being a time of disruption, the Balkan Wars dramatically changed the outlook for both native and missionary assessment of goals and plans for the future.

The other important limitation of this study is that it considers only one American missionary organization. Similar missionary work conducted by a Methodist society is not discussed here. The intent is to concentrate upon the American Board and its Bulgarian involvement.

This study is based primarily on three archival collections: the official archives of the American Board (kept in the Houghton Library, Harvard University) and two private collections of prominent missionary families—the Clarkes and the Haskells. The latter two archives only recently became available for scholarly use through the efforts of the Hilandar Research Library. Thus far they have not been utilized in related historiography, a circumstance which allows the present research to incorporate previously unavailable primary sources. (It should be noted that these archives are largely unorganized and have not yet been cataloged.) Other relevant documentary materials were also studied as supplementary sources. These represent primarily American and Bulgarian periodicals, particularly those of missionary origin, and occasional memoirs by contemporaries. Special effort was taken to research the limited number of Bulgarian sources which are usually ignored by English-speaking scholars of the subject.

The existing historiography on the American Board's involvement among the Bulgarians is rather limited but nevertheless useful in the assessment of various aspects of the problem under study. In English there are only two monographs which deal exclusively with the subject. Both are doctoral dissertations from the 1930's. The first, *Bible Societies, American Missionaries and the National Revival of Bulgaria,* by J. F. Clark,(1) is especially valuable for the study of both the early missionary experience in the country as well as the history of the publishing of the Scriptures in modern Bulgarian. W. W. Hall's work, *Puritans in the Balkans,*(2) is an excellent narrative study of the American Board's experience in Bulgaria in the period 1878-1918. Since this work offers much first hand information, it is occasionally useful as a primary source.

More recently, another doctoral dissertation dealt with the history of the American Board in the Balkan Peninsula as a part of a larger study. P. B. Mojzes' "A History of the Congregational and Methodist Churches in Bulgaria and Yugoslavia" appeared in 1965.(3) This work represents a narrative rather than interpretive history of the religious aspects of missionary work.

Another major group of studies which aid the discussion of the present problem is the various histories of American missionary activities in general. Among these, the works of Rufus Anderson, Robert Daniel, James Field, Jr., Joseph Grabill, and William Strong are important.(4) Each contains a small section dealing with certain aspects of the American Board Bulgarian mission.

The relevant Bulgarian historiography is less impressive in quantity and substance. There are only two articles in Bulgarian which specifically discuss the experience of the American Board in general. These works, authored by Man'o Stoi͡anov and by Petŭr Shopov, were published in 1964 and 1974, respectively.(5) Stoi͡anov discusses the beginning of the missionary enterprise in Bulgaria, and Shopov deals with the same subject during the second half of the nineteenth century. Neither work relies on missionary archival materials, which is characteristic of most other Bulgarian scholarly publications relating to this topic. By taking into account existing Bulgarian historiography, an important gap in the English language literature on the subject is closed, as the latter in principle ignores the related Bulgarian scholarly writings.

One major difficultly encountered in this research stemmed from the fact that the Bulgarians used the Julian Calendar until March 31, 1916. The missionaries who resided there, as a rule, used the Gregorian Calendar, and their correspondence and official reports are dated accordingly. Therefore, all dates in the present study are given according to the Gregorian style. One notable exception is the publishing dates of Bulgarian newspapers which could not be changed since they are a major source of reference. It should be kept in mind, therefore, that in referring to *Zorni͡tsa, Makedonii͡a* and *Tur͡tsii͡a*, dating according to the Julian style was preserved.

In transliterating Bulgarian names and words in general, the transliteration system of the Library of Congress for Bulgarian was applied. All translations from Bulgarian into English are the work of this author.

Finally, I would like to acknowledge my appreciation of Mrs. Esther N. Clarke and the Haskell family for making available the Clarke and Haskell Papers. I also thank the

Hilandar Research Library of the Ohio State University for copying these papers and making them available to me. These collections contributed much to the preparation of this project. I also thank Ms. Nancy Grace for her expert editing and Dr. Richard Hall for his kindness in drawing the map. Most of all, I would like to express gratitude to my advisor, Dr. Carole Rogel, for her guidance and encouragement and to my husband, Predrag, for his strong support throughout this time.

References to Introduction

1. James F. Clarke, *Bible Societies, American Missionaries and the National Revival of Bulgaria*, (New York: Arno Press & The New York Times, 1971).

2. William Webster Hall, Jr., *Puritans in the Balkans. The American Board Mission in Bulgaria, 1878-1918: A Study in Purpose and Procedure*, (Studia Historico-Philologica Serdicensia, Supplementi Vol. 1, Sofia, 1938).

3. Paul Benjamin Mojzes, "A History of the Congregational and Methodist Churches in Bulgaria and Yugoslavia," (Ph.D. dissertation, Boston University, 1965).

4. Rufus Anderson, *History of the Missions of the American Board of Commissioners for Foreign Missions to the Oriental Churches*, 2 vols., (Boston: Congregational Publishing Society, 1872); Robert L. Daniel, *American Philanthropy in the Near East 1820-1960*, (Athens, Ohio: Ohio University Press, 1969); Joseph L. Grabill, *Protestant Diplomacy and the Near East. Missionary Influence on American Policy, 1810-1927,* (Minneapolis: University of Minnesota Press, 1971); William E. Strong, *The Story of the American Board of Commissioners for Foreign Missions*, (Boston, New York, Chicago: The Pilgrim Press, 1910).

5. Man'o Stoi͡anov, "Nachalo na protestantskata propaganda v Bŭlgarii͡a," *Izvestii͡a na Instituta za istorii͡a* 14-15:45-67; Petŭr Shopov, "Propagandnata i prosvetna deinost na amerikanskite bibleiski obshtestva v bŭlgarskite zemi prez XIX v.," *Izvestii͡a na Instituta za istorii͡a* 23:149-184.

CHAPTER I
DIRECT EFFORTS TOWARDS EVANGELIZING THE BULGARIANS

1. *The American Board "Discovers" the Bulgarians*

The American Board's involvement with the Bulgarians came as a result of its general interest and activity in the Near East*. The missionary organization represented the Congregational and the Presbyterian Churches** in America and was formed in 1810. Only nine years after its birth, the American Board sent two of its missionaries to the Near East. In 1819, Pliny Fisk and Levi Parsons arrived in Smyrna, beginning a period of more than a century during which time continuous efforts were made to spread Protestantism in that region. In the course of these endeavors, the Americans "discovered" a people, the Bulgarians, who at first seemed to need the Protestant message and appeared willing to receive it. Initial contacts between the missionaries of the American Board and the Bulgarians occurred at the most dynamic and crucial time of Bulgarian history. Following a series of defeats, the Bulgarians had lost their independence to the Turks in 1396 and for the next five centuries continued to exist within the framework of the Ottoman Empire. From the beginning of the eighteenth century to 1878, when a significant number of them gained independence, the Bulgarians were undergoing the so called "period of National Revival." A leading contemporary Bulgarian historian of this period briefly defined it as ". . .a part of the general European process which accomplished the transition from the Middle Ages to the bourgeois world."(1) One of the peculiar features of this process among the Bulgarians was the fact that it was at the

*In this study, Near East refers to the Ottoman Empire and its successor States, Persia, the Caucasus, and the Balkans.

** The Presbyterian Churches withdrew from the American Board in 1870.

same time a "process of the ripening, preparation and accomplishment of the Bulgarian national-liberation... revolution."(2) The manifestations of the Revival movement could be detected in all spheres of Bulgarian life—social, economic, political, cultural, religious.

In learning about the Bulgarians as a separate and distinct nationality in the Ottoman Empire, the American missionaries were aided by representatives of the British and Foreign Bible Society*. As James F. Clarke has established, this society in its efforts to produce a Bulgarian New Testament became a critical instrument in drawing the attention of the missionaries to the Bulgarian population.(3) As early as 1826, an agent of the British and Foreign Bible Society, Benjamin Barker, reported that there was a definite need for "the Sacred Scriptures in the Bulgarian language."(4) In 1840 the same agent, after travelling in the Bulgarian lands, voiced the opinion that this territory was an inviting field for missionary activity.(5) This information was passed on to the Americans, and it even reached the pages of the *Missionary Herald* that same year.

The missionaries of the American Board made their own tours and reported similar views. H. G. O. Dwight and W. G. Schauffler probably first made known the Board's interest in the Bulgarian population. Following a tour of European Turkey in 1834, the two missionaries concluded that a mission in that part of the empire was sorely needed. However, they did not specifically mention the Bulgarians.(6) In 1841, H. J. van Lennep, a commercial agent for the American missionaries in Smyrna, voiced great enthusiasm about the prospects of missionary involvement with the Bulgarians. He based his argument for the need of such work on the fact that at a certain fair nearly two thousand New Testaments in Bulgarian were sold in less than a week.(7)Another missionary, H. A. Homes, wrote to the American Board that "a mission among the Bulgarians is more called for than among any other people who have not yet had missionaries."(8) Bulgaria seemed to him the most promising field in the entire Ottoman Empire.(9)

* The society was formed in 1804 in London for the purpose of universally distributing the Scriptures.

In the early 1840's, again, the eminent missionary to the Greeks, Elias Riggs, became acquainted with the Bulgarian language and also thought that missionary work among the Bulgarians was desirable.(10) He specifically mentioned in his memoirs that in the summer of 1844, during a visit by Rufus Anderson, Secretary of the American Board, "those of us who were in the Greek department pleaded. . .for the prosecution of work for the Bulgarians."(11) The repeatedly expressed interest in establishing a Bulgarian mission did not result in anything substantial since the American Board was discouraged by the difficulties met in its work among the Greeks. As James F. Clarke pointed out, the latter endeavor proved to have a direct impact on the missionary Bulgarian initiative.(12) In addition, the experience of the American Board resulting from its involvement with the Armenian population within the Ottoman Empire was another factor that directly benefitted the subsequent missionary work among the Bulgarians. Another scholar, W. W. Hall, Jr., initially emphasized this circumstance.(13)

In the early 1850's, the American Board manifested a continuing interest in the Bulgarians and gathered information about them from its representatives who were already laboring among the Greeks and the Armenians.(14) No real steps for initiating missionary work among the Bulgarians were considered, however, until 1856 when Cyrus Hamlin*, one of the most well-known missionaries of the American Board, travelled to the United States on commission from the Constantinople Station with the goal "to press upon the secretaries of the Board the necessity of a mission to the Bulgarians."(15) The American Board decided to act but in cooperation with the Methodist Episcopal Church. The lack of sufficient financial means made it practical to divide the Bulgarian lands into two fields for missionary work with the Balkan Mountains serving as a boundary. The American Board was to proceed with its Bulgarian involvement to the south of that mountain range.(16) On his way back to Turkey, Hamlin spent some time in London where the Turkish Missions Aid Society** encouraged his initiative. Once again,

* Cyrus Hamlin (1811-1900) later became known as the founder of Robert College.

** This British society financially aided the American Board with its Turkish missions.

the English Protestants were extremely helpful in supporting the American interest in the Bulgarian population. At the beginning of American missionary involvement with the Bulgarians, this British society offered financial help to the American Board. The President of the society, the Earl of Shaftesbury, wrote Hamlin in June, 1856, stating that "... Bulgaria would be a fruitful field for the labors of evangelical missionaries."(17) In addition, he suggested that the society would provide "say three hundred pounds a year"(18) to maintain two missionaries of the American Board to the Bulgarians.

In May of the following year, Hamlin together with an English traveller,* went on an exploratory tour of the Bulgarian lands south of the Balkan Mountains. His report of the tour was quite favorable and the Bulgarian mission of the American board was initiated following its adoption.(19) The first station of the Board was established on July 16, 1858** in Adrianople where Rev. Charles Morse and his wife settled and were later joined by Rev. Theodore L. Byington and his wife.(20) These events marked the beginning of nearly a century of uninterrupted efforts by missionaries of the American Board to evangelize the Bulgarians.

2. *Goals and Methods Used by the American Board in Its Work among the Bulgarians (1858-1870)*

The first misionaries to the Bulgarians sent by the American Board were appointed to work under the so-called Western Turkey Mission. Their general aim was typical of any Christian missionary organization or individual. In the words of one of the best known American missionaries to Bulgaria, Rev. James F. Clarke,***"The problem to be solved here (i.e.,

* This Englishman was the Rev. Henry Jones, who afterwards became the secretary of the Turkish Missions Aid Society; see William E. Strong, *The Story of the American Board*, (Boston, New York, Chicago: The Pilgrim Press, 1910), p. 308.

** This date was found in documents in the Clarke Papers. All historiography on the subject thus far, including my Master's thesis, gives March as the founding date. See, for example, Hall, p. 72 and Mojzes, p. 64.

*** Not to be confused with his grandson and well-known historian, the late Prof. James F. Clarke, some of whose works have been mentioned in this study.

in Bulgaria) as everywhere is the salvation of souls."(21) The ways of achieving this, however, were naturally influenced by conditions in Bulgarian society at the time. The period of the 1850s was characterized by a particularly active struggle on behalf of the Bulgarians for an independent church. With the coming of Turkish rule in Bulgaria, the Bulgarian Church was placed under the authority of the Byzantine Patriarch in Constantinople. Centuries later the movement to free Bulgarians from Greek ecclesiastical rule became one of the main components of the Bulgarian National Revival*.

When the missionaries of the American Board arrived in Southern Bulgaria, they found themselves immersed in an atmosphere of intense struggle for the creation of a Bulgarian national church. They had to cope with this issue and to take sides, aligning against the Greek clergy and supporting the Bulgarian claims.(22) To the missionaries, this seemed a great opportunity to reform the entire Bulgarian population and its national church organization. As one of them explained, "... we should labor for the salvation of the Bulgarians in their church, in distinction from laboring with the expectation that separate Protestant communities would be formed in time."(23) This ambitious goal probably resulted not only from the proselytizing nature of any missionary enterprise but also from an incorrect evaluation of the religious struggle in Bulgaria. Many years later, a prominent Bulgarian evangelist, A. S. T͡sanov, remembered that an American missionary saw the initial work of the Protestants as intended to help the Bulgarians in their struggle with the Greek Patriarchate.(24) In 1864, the Rev. James F. Clarke also explained to the natives of the town of Kalofer that the missionaries "do not come to ask you /the Bulgarians/ to leave your church, but to receive the Bible and live by it in the church."(25) Obviously, the pioneers of Protestantism among the Bulgarians considered that, to a significant degree, the goals of Americans and natives coincided as far as the struggle for an independent Bulgarian church was concerned.

These high hopes were shaken to a certain extent in the early 1860's when it became clear that the leaders of the

* For details about the struggle for an independent Bulgarian Church see P. Nikov, *Vŭzrazhdane na bŭlgarskii͡a narod. Tsŭrkovno-nat͡sionalni borbi i postizhenii͡a*, Sofia, 1929.

Bulgarian movement for an independent church would decide to join the Protestant millet* only as a political move aimed at gaining their much sought religious independence.(26) Still, the original plan of the missionaries lingered on during the early 1870's. Bulgarian independence in church affairs was finally gained with the establishment of the Bulgarian Orthodox Exarchate in February, 1870. The missionaries met this event with a continuing, but not as confident, expectation that they could reform church life in Bulgaria along Protestant lines. Thus, Henry C. Haskell, a missionary stationed at Philippopolis /present-day Plovdiv/ wrote: "Is there not reason to hope that this nominal division of the Bulgarians from the Greek Church, may ultimately contribute to the conversion of the nation to Christ?"(27) During that same year, the December issue of *Missionary Herald* offered the hope of reforming the Bulgarian church as one of two possible ways of accomplishing the missionary task. Thus, the establishment of the Bulgarian Exarchate is considered

> to give reason to hope that the use of proper Christian influence will lead to an early acceptance of a purer Christianity, and result in either the formation of independent Protestant churches, or a renovation of the Bulgarian church.(28)

Since the original idea of the American Board was quite ambitious and, according to one historian, contained "a certain amount of arrogance and presumption,"(29) the initial methods of achieving it were designed not to offend or alienate the masses of Orthodox Bulgarians. The *Missionary Herald* characterized these methods as intended "to present the great truths of salvation rather than to attack openly the errors of the church."(30) Todor Ikonomov, one of the fierce opponents of missionary involvement among the Bulgarians and a leading Bulgarian figure, remembered with a feeling of nostalgia the early missionaries who did not immediately challenge the traditional values held dear by native population. In a book aiming to discredit the American missionaries in Bulgaria, Ikonomov emphasized that the first

* The Protestant millet was recognized by the Grand Vizier in November 1847 and gave civil legal status to all Protestants in the Ottoman Empire.

Protestants who came to work among his people did it "with a certain caution, with a delicateness which did not so sharply offend our national feeling or our religious orientation."(31) The missionaries spent their first years among the Bulgarians with the desire not to create a confrontation but to work within the framework of the existing local church organizations. Because of that tack, the Americans repeateadly insisted that the creation of Protestant civil communities among the Bulgarians "should be deferred as long as possible."(32) They did not wish to create divisions among the natives but to work for the conversion of the entire population.

Keeping their final goal in mind and attempting to emphasize the common features between Orthodoxy and Protestantism, the men and women sent by the American Board settled among the Bulgarians. Their actual behavior was determined by one model for conversion—to approach the natives individually and to convince them of the truth of the Protestant message. In the words of the Rev. James F. Clarke, the way to achieve the lofty goal of salvation of souls was "by preaching the gospel directly...to each individual."(33) In practice, this translated into attempts to reach as many Bulgarians as possible and to develop good relations with the leading men among them. Once the missionaries were settled at a location, which for the American Board became one of its stations, they usually spent the first year learning the language and getting acquainted with the place and its surroundings. Such was the case in Adrianople, in Philippopolis, in Eski Zagra (present-day Stara Zagora) and in Sofia, where stations were established between 1858 and 1862.(34) The missionaries usually went to the Orthodox churches and to the schools to meet people. In Philippopolis, they even went for Sunday services to the Orthodox church of the Virgin Mary.(35) Once the Americans had a sufficient grasp of the Bulgarian language, they would actively engage in preaching any place where they might encounter Bulgarians. Charles F. Morse, who initiated the Sofia station, describes this in his first annual report: "We have no service but go out on the Sabbath. . .and converse with whomsoever we can find."(36) A Sofia resident by the name of Kosta Mikhailov recorded information about Morse's activity which presents a more complete picture of the actual manner in which the missionaries behaved. According to Mikhailov, when Morse settled in Sofia he "boldly preached even in the church /obviously, the Orthodox church/...untiringly /he/ was lecturing and preaching at fairs, in shops and in homes,...and was giving out different books and booklets."(37)

Some of the favorite places for initiating and even maintaining Protestant preaching were the coffee-shops where Bulgarian males customarily congregated. This was especially true at times of touring when the Americans, usually accompanied by native helpers, would attempt to spread their influence in the surrounding areas. Henry C. Haskell entered in his journal the following description of his stay in the town of Klisura in March 1864: "Talked and sang some hymns in a coffee-room. Sang for an hour at school. P.M. visited other coffee-rooms and talked, sang and sold a few books."(38) The coffee-shop was used even for conducting prayers, as was the case of the village of Bansko where in the late 1860's native converts met to pray on Sundays.(39)

Certainly the Americans and their helpers were visible to their potential converts and/or enemies and, in fact, the representatives of the American Board always thought of ways to increase this visibility and present their teachings in attractive forms. In order to gain acceptance amongst the natives, for example, the missionaries in Eski Zagra offered to give English lessons to the young men during 1861, but apparently after taking a few lessons, the Bulgarians gave it up. Following this setback, the missionaries "endeavored to attract them by spending a short time before service in teaching them to sing Bulgarian hymns."(40) This innovation was also short-lived, but the Americans continued, especially after 1870, to use more and different approaches to attract the attention of the native population.

The first twelve years of the American Board's involvement among the Bulgarians were obviously years of ambitious aims and cautious approaches. The work proceeded without a formal separation of individual converts but with a definite plan to evangelize the native Orthodox church and thus to accomplish the salvation of the overwhelming majority of the Bulgarian population. With the slow gain in converts, however, and with the gradual acquisition of firsthand knowledge about their field, the missionaries had to deal with some important problems. One was the need to protect and cultivate their followers. Another was the growing awareness that the fulfillment of their mission would not come soon. In the course of those first twelve years, the Americans were faced with difficulties which naturally could not be foreseen. To meet the challenges of real everyday missionary life, they had to adapt initial ideas, to change methods and to introduce new ones. The final goal remained unchanged, but the realities of the missionary enterprise in the Bulgarian lands produced various new short-term goals and ways of achieving them.

3. *The European Turkey Mission: Goals, Methods, Organization*

The first major changes came in the early 1870's and concerned questions of organization. Due to their increased involvement among the Bulgarians and the experience gained in the course of the years, the missionaries arrived at the idea that a separate mission to the Bulgarians should be constituted and thus their formal connection with the Western Turkey Mission should be terminated. The suggestion came at a convention of those missionaries who worked among the Bulgarian population. The convention, held in Philippopolis in March 1869, adopted the following resolution: "...it is desirable that the Mission to W. Turkey, at its next annual meeting constitute. . .a separate mission to be called the Bulgarian mission."(41) More importantly, this resolution was made a reality the following year. The work among the Bulgarians and the missionaries conducting it were obviously considered mature enough to continue on their own. On May 27, 1870 during the 30th annual meeting of the Western Turkey mission, the missionary stations at Eski Zagra, Philippopolis, Samokov*, Adrianople and Constantinople** were constituted as a separate mission "to be called the European Turkey Mission."(42) Even though the name of the originally proposed mission was changed, all essential features

* The Sofia Station was abandoned in favor of Samokov, where a station was initiated in 1869; see J. F. C. 63/1, p. 1, Clarke Papers.

** Constantinople belonged to the European Turkey Mission so far as it was related to the Bulgarian work; see endnote 43.

of the resolution of 1869 were retained. The newly created mission represented an organizational change that marked the start of other innovations in the entire missionary enterprise in Bulgaria. The most important of these new developments was the formation of the first separate Protestant church among the Bulgarians. This episode occurred on August 27, 1871, in Bansko where a church of 15 members with a Bulgarian pastor, I. A. Tondzhorov*, was inaugurated.(43) The most significant feature of this event was the fact that it plainly contradicted the expressed policy against the formation of separate Protestant communities /religious or civil/. Obviously, events in the Bulgarian lands had moved ahead of initial missionary planning. However, the formation of that first native Protestant church was not discussed anywhere in missionary writing as contradictory to the original goals of reforming the Bulgarian Orthodox Church.

Throughout the remaining period before the Balkan Wars, the Americans, both workers in Bulgaria and their superiors at the headquarters of the American Board in Boston, continued to have definite aspirations for the overall evangelization of the Bulgarians by influencing their traditional church. In 1894, for example, when the missionaries were able to report the existence of 14 Protestant churches in their field, (44) they were still hoping to exercise a decisive influence upon the Bulgarian Orthodox Church. On the pages of a missionary publication coming out of Samokov, an anonymous author shared the following desire:

> And may we not hope for the exertion of such an influence on the Pravo-Slav /i.e., Orthodox/ church as shall lead it to drop its most unchristian usages. . .to introduce preaching into its Sunday services, and in general to become more evangelical in Spirit?"

These expectations were set in a definite time framework, with the much wished for results to become reality in the next twenty years.(45)

During July 1894, H. C. Haskell visited the town of Prilep and commented on the final goal of reforming the Orthodox

* In most American sources the name Tondzhorov is incorrectly transcribed as Tonzhorov.

Church in the Bulgarian lands. In his mind, that end could be accomplished most effectively by the influence of the existing Protestant churches:

> On coming it was quite a problem in my mind whether the Kingdom wld best be served by trying to form a separate ch. here or by trying to strengthen the spiritual forces in the old. ch. . . ./now convinced/ that a separate Evang. Ch. will secure the salvation of more men and will sooner accomplish a reformation in the old ch. than any other means.(46)

There was not even a mention of the fact that the formation of Protestant churches and the reformation of the Orthodox Church were previously considered two incompatible goals. These two options were now regarded as complementing each other, and the formation of Protestant churches was viewed only as a means to accomplish the larger aim. Some missionaries expressed doubts, but the idea of evangelizing the native church was never taken out of consideration.

This lack of clarity in terms of the most appropriate way of accomplishing the missionary objective was, perhaps, most clearly expressed in a letter by J. F. Clarke, dated April 30, 1881. Answering a letter from N. G. Clark, the Secretary of the American Board in Boston, the missionary had to report on "how far has the character of the old Bulgarian church improved in respect to its morals and ceremonies and the use of the Scriptures."(47) Not seeing any "improvement" J. F. Clarke voiced the opinion that advanced among the Bulgarians "is not *in the church*, but rather in spite of it... Our hope for the renovation of the Bulgarian people is rather in the Evangelical Society* which is showing increased vitality (Clarke's emphasis)."(48) This is one of the few instances when a missionary so clearly expressed complete disbelief in the possibility of reforming the native church. Otherwise, that goal continued to be held as a realistic and valid one to the end of the period under consideration. In 1906, for instance, the Secretary of the American Board, James L. Barton, posed almost a rhetorical question as if reprimanding missionary

* Clarke had in mind the Bulgarian Evangelical Society which was formed in 1875 after the model of American home missionary societies.

actions that lacked clarity and proper perspective: "I wonder how much the mission is working for a reform in the old church rather than for separation from the old Church into the Protestant body."(49) He recognized the obvious contradictory nature of those two options. Again, however, Barton gave clear preference to the original plan of reforming the existing native church by offering practical advice concerning the first steps in accomplishing that missionary task.(50) Furthermore, in the annual report of the American Board from that same year, the missionaries emphasized the temporary character of the Protestant churches called into being by their work:

> While Protestantism as a distinct organization may not be making much progress, evangelical truth is spreading, and it is due to the influence of Protestantism that there are. . .quickenings in the national life /of Bulgarians/.(51)

Those organizations were definitely viewed as the vehicle by which to influence the majority of the native population. The lack of decisive growth in that respect, therefore, was not considered a fatal symptom of the final goal. The discouraging results of the efforts at evangelization left no room for a choice. The missionaries had to hope that the Bulgarian "nation would be truly evangelized and that meanwhile, till the national church be quickened, the distinctive Protestant element must and will be maintained."(52) The conflict between the high goal held by the missionaries and the apparently unsatisfactory results continued to be resolved in that manner to the end of missionary engagement among the Bulgarians. Doubts as to how to accomplish that goal did not diminish the firm belief that the evangelization of Bulgaria would occur. The general tendency was to seek favorable changes in the official Orthodox Church and to consider the existing separate Protestant churches as an instrument, as an example for making these changes possible. The contradictions between reality and ambitious goals were resolved in that manner in missionary thinking which gave hope not only for the distant future but also for the present when Protestantism could not claim more than 1,500 church members in Southern Bulgaria.(53)

The contrast between the vision of evangelical Bulgaria and the insignificant numerical results of their work was the main reason why the missionaries were reluctant to take steps toward the formation of separate civil communities by the native Protestants. The Americans, naturally, did not want to see further division among a people they expected to evangelize extensively. Given the conditions within the Turkish Empire and later within the framework of semi-independent Bulgaria, the missionaries attempted to proceed with their work but not to encourage the formation of civil Protestant communities. At the third annual meeting of the European Turkey Mission during May-June of 1873, a resolution was passed confirming the policy that it was not considered "expedient to form Prot. Communities provided their /the Bulgarians/ political rights can be otherwise secured."(54)

The dilemma was a difficult one—to protect the limited number of converts and at the same time not to isolate them further from the rest of the native population. The conflict between the reality of a small Protestant community and the final goal of evangelizing the entire field found another expression in this resolution which had the tendency to sacrifice the immediate interests of the few converts for the sake of a vision of an evangelized Southern Bulgaria. The same decision was upheld at the ninth annual meeting of the Mission in 1880, and it was defended in a letter to the American Board by one of the missionaries, E. W. Jenny:

> for the sake of the /Bulgarian/ national desire for unity and the evil effects of separating politically from the Orthodox, especially on the inhabitants of Macedonia,* we deem it decisively unwise to draw a political line of distinction which shall in any way prejudice /sic/ the people against us.(55)

The Americans, worried that they might alienate potential converts, i.e., any Bulgarian, did not seek the creation of a formal Bulgarian component to the Protestant millet in Turkey. For the Bulgarians who lived in the newly formed Bulgarian Principality with its constitutional system guar-

* The region remained under Turkish rule after the Russo-Turkish War of 1877-1878 and the subsequent formation of the Principality of Bulgaria.

anteeing religious freedom, this policy was never changed, but for those who remained in Turkish territory the missionaries felt an obligation to assure Protestant converts better protection from the general hostility shown toward them.

The initiative for change came by the Bulgarian Protestants in Bansko, the birthplace of the first Bulgarian evangelical church sanctioned by the American Board. As announced in the annual report of the Samokov Station for 1881-1882, "our friends have applied for and obtained an order setting them off into a Prot. civil Comty." The reason for this action, which clearly did not fit existing missionary policies, was that the Protestants in Bansko could no longer endure "oppression of many kinds specially from their own people on account of their faith."(56) Conditions in the Ottoman Empire did not lend themselves to expediency in administrative matters; hence, it took about a year for actual recognition by the government. The exact date is not mentioned in the reports, but sometime toward the end of 1882 the Protestant community in Bansko was consolidated under its own representative and was officially recognized by the Turks.

In addition, "the other Protestant Communities upon the Razlog Plain. . .have been recognized as separate communities and been allowed to pay their taxes through their own representatives." The missionary writing that report, J. H. House, added with a touch of apprehension that the Bulgarians "seem to be much pleased with the new arrangement, but of course experience alone will show whether it is as desirable as it seems to be."(57) Once more pressures by the actual conditions of work among the Bulgarians forced changes in clearly stated missionary policies. And once more the change was not discussed but simply stated. Curiously, this change was not approved or even mentioned in the subsequent annual meetings of the Mission. The missionaries obviously did not wholeheartedly support the innovation, but their obligations to the converts among the Bulgarians could no longer stall the native desire for real protection. So division along political lines became a reality for the Bulgarians who remained in the Ottoman Empire. In practical terms, this meant a separate payment of taxes and separate settlement of all civil matters.

The continuing involvement among the Bulgarians presented the European Turkey Mission with an increasing variety of tasks. The constant goal of gaining new converts was parallelled gradually with the natural necessity to direct and influence in an appropriate manner the group of native professing Protestants. An understandable need existed to think about ways of keeping the Bulgarian evangelists properly organized and mobilized. As a rule, these people were members of separate Protestant churches modeled after any typical American congregational church. In the words of W. W. Hall:

> The churches which the missionaries called into being in Bulgaria were founded upon general Congregationalist principles. They were to consist only of those committed to a Christian way of life with an experiential knowledge of the faith which they professed; they were to provide an educated ministry and raise up a schooled and enlightened laity; each church was to be a free, self-governing, democratically controlled unit.(58)

These basic principles were formulated and gradually adopted by the slowly increasing number of Protestant churches in Southern Bulgaria. The idea was to unify and standardize this basic form of organization among the native followers. For example, in the late 1880's, a constitution for all evangelical Bulgarian churches in the field of the American Board was prepared and adopted by representatives of these churches. This occurred at a general conference which met in the city of Pazardzhik in May 1888.(59) Following the conference, the individual churches received and eventually adopted the document. In the region of the Philippopolis Station, this procedure was completed in the course of roughly a year, (60) and this was probably the case in the rest of the field even though specific mention to that effect has not been found.

A greater degree of uniformity was achieved toward the end of the period under discussion. In 1909, all the evangelical churches in the now Kingdom of Bulgaria* were able to agree

* On October 5, 1908, the ruler of Bulgaria, Prince Ferdinand, proclaimed the independence of the country and was crowned the King of Bulgaria.

upon one common set of regulations governing their internal life. This was accomplished in October at an Evangelical Congress in Sofia.(61) The meeting represented not only churches which came into existence under the direction of the American Board but all churches of Protestant background. Nevertheless, it was certainly a good indicator of the successful effort by the missionaries sent from Boston to make Bulgarian Protestantism a uniformly organized institution. The congress could, in addition, be regarded as proof of the maturity of the native Protestants who certainly did not overemphasize denominational differences. This quality was carefully cultivated by the missionaries of the American Board whose goal was to prepare a confident and competent native Protestant force. In the mid-1870's, for example, the Americans started to consult with their Bulgarian followers in a formal manner. Obviously intending to expose the natives to the process of decision-making in the missionary field, the Americans invited some native workers to serve on a committee at the fifth annual meeting of the European Turkey Mission in July 1875. The committee had the task of preparing a list of salaries to be paid to the native appointees of the American Board.(62) Gradually throughout the next two decades, the idea of regular meetings among natives and missionaries evolved and was put into practice. The first general conference "of workers from all parts of the field" was organized in July 1883, again in connection with the consecutive annual meeting of the Mission.

The next two years witnessed two smaller gatherings at the station level in connection with the work in the Samokov area, and in 1888 another regional conference took place in Bansko.(63) A new development occurred at a meeting of the Bulgarian Evangelical Society in 1888 when the society adopted a system of regular permanent conferences. All churches that came into being as a result of the American Board's activity were divided into three groups or church conferences:

> the 'Razlog' in Bansko and surrounding places, chiefly in the Razlog district; the 'Central', including Sophia, Samokov and vicinity; and the 'Eastern Bulgarian' for Philippopolis and places connected with that city.(64)

The first meetings of the newly established church conferences were held in October-November 1889.(65)

Clearly the missionaries in European Turkey were applying a new organizational approach which assured the development of a competent native leadership and a good measure of native contribution to the missionary enterprise. In spite of indications that the Bulgarian Protestants "looked with a good deal of indifference" upon the initial establishment of church conferences,(66) they remained a permanent institution and even began to meet annually in the early 1890's. Thus, in October 1891 the three conferences gathered in separate places, and the following year new meetings were held in October and November. At that time, participants of the Razlog Conferences planned to hold their meetings semiannually.(67) In April 1893, a general conference of all evangelical churches connected with the American Board was held, and conference members chose Marko N. Popov as formal representative to the government.(68) This method of organizing the native Protestants was clearly working to bring the Bulgarian converts together and to keep them active. The missionaries themselves valued the new feature of their work which they considered as evidence "of Christian development and growth in the Bulgarian evangelical churches."(69) The practice of regular gatherings continued to be an established feature of the life of the Bulgarian Protestants.(70)

The missionaries also used other means at times to keep native workers active and competent in their task. These workers would often undergo training classes which were usually called "summer school." The practice began in 1883 when the Mission originated a separate department for Bible work headed by Ellen M. Stone. The workers in this department were women whose task was to teach native women to read and learn from the Bible and other Christian literature.(71) The Bulgarian women who staffed this branch of the missionary enterprise were usually not well educated, particularly in the beginning, and needed extra schooling. Answering that need, the missionaries organized annual summer classes for them in Samokov which was the educational center of the Mission. The first training session of this kind took place in May 1886, and lasted for four weeks.(72) In addition to this regular training, which continued until the departure of Miss Stone in 1902,* the missionaries occasionally offered summer schooling for their native helpers; such was the case in August 1986, when male and female workers participated, and in July 1910, when participants were women who worked for the Protestant cause in Southern Bulgaria.(73) All training classes continued to be held in Samokov. Coupled with the practice of holding annual conferences, the organization of summer school sessions represented one of the primary missionary activities relating to the care of the Protestant converts.

The problem of reaching new potential followers was equally, if not more, important. The basic approach to this task did not differ much from the initial missionary practice of individual conversions. With the gradual establishment of small Protestant communities, however, the Americans were able to apply other well-known methods of work, such as revivalism which was popular in their own country. The first significant wave of revival meetings in the European Turkey Mission came as a result of a similar movement in all of the Turkish missions of the American Board.(74) In March 1883, the missionaries in Samokov started daily prayer meetings which resulted in "a remarkable religious interest, such as has never been known here."(75) The revival movement spread to the other stations in the Southern Bulgarian lands and the same techniques of reaching the native population were often used by the missionaries throughout the 1912-1913 period.(76)

The efficacy of the revival movement is difficult to evaluate since the statistics left by the missionaries do not show any significant increase in the number of new church members during times of pronounced revivalism. The same statistics, however, indicate that the average number of churchgoers increased during these same periods. For example, in 1883, the average size of the congregations increased over 14% During years without revivals, similar increases were not found.(77) Significant growth was noted in other years when strong revivalist movement was experienced,(78) a fact which indicates that this method of reaching more and more

* Ellen Stone became something of an international celebrity following her abduction in the summer of 1901 by revolutionaries in Macedonia. For details see Laura Beth Sherman, *Fires on the Mountain*, (Boulder, Colorado: East European Monographs, 1980).

Bulgarians worked at least partially. While the actual number of church members did not increase, the number of people who heard the Protestant message definitely rose.

With the same goal in mind — to reach the greatest possible number of Bulgarians — the missionaries attempted to change some of their traditional ways of practicing Christianity. In the spring of 1882, for instance, they sanctioned the inauguration of "open-air services" by one of the best native preachers.(79) However, the innovation soon proved a failure due surprisingly to the opposition of the native Protestants, some of whom were "timid," some "ashamed," and some showed "so little appreciation of the spirit of the gospel as to charge the leaders in this movement with fanaticism."(80) Clearly, this method proved to be rather bold for the small group of Bulgarian converts, and the missionaries soon abandoned it, thus once more illustrating the basic contradiction in all missionary activity — the contradiction between their goal of converting all Bulgarians to Protestantism and the reality of the insignificant numerical results of their work. In this case, the Americans had to accommodate the feelings of their followers at the expense of possibly gaining new converts at the open-air services.

In the spring of 1910, another innovation was tried by one of the younger missionaries, Edward B. Haskell. He attempted to make known the missionary message by means of delivering public lectures to large audiences. This "novel experiment for reaching as large a number of people as possible" took place in the city of Salonica* /i.e., Thessaloniki/.(81) The lectures were usually on popular religious subjects and created considerable interest. The very first lecture drew an audience of 500 people. The new method indicated a growing tendency to popularize Protestant ideas, as opposed to the initial missionary methods that emphasized the individual approach.

The search for new ways of achieving the major goal of evangelizing the Bulgarians included the repeated use of different attractions which brought otherwise unreachable people to the missionaries. The missionaries noticed that when

* Salonica became a station of the European Turkey Mission in October/November 1894. It should be noted that some of the mission stations are not a part of present-day Bulgarian territory (Monastir and Salonica, in particular), but they were nevertheless working for Bulgarians.

something unusual or unknown was added to their preaching the audiences dramatically increased. In January 1871, for instance, the station in Eski Zagra received a cabinet organ for use in the work of evangelizing. As one of the missionaries wrote, "We exhibit it with pride to all visitors, as a triumph of American skill."(82) Of course, the feelings of patriotism on this occasion were important but even more so was the realization that, as W. W. Sleeper wrote in 1884, the organ would further the missionary goals. In an attempt to defend the desire of the missionaries in Samokov to order a small organ /the so called "baby-organ"/ from the United States, Sleeper wrote to the American Board:

> The Bulgarian preachers assure me that it /the organ/ would draw large audiences, and hold them, too. It would assist in worship, besides being a great attraction. I want to utilize to the utmost the great love for music with which this people is gifted.(83)

The missionaries certainly tried to accommodate the peculiarities of the people in this particular field. At the same time, they realized that the organs were an attraction for the natives. For the Americans, however, the end result was of greater importance and, in fact, they actively pursued such additional means at their disposal to enhance the importance of the Protestant message. The Samokov station received a small organ, indeed, and in its annual report for 1884-1885 it was once again emphasized, this time from first hand experience, that "this people can be attracted and held more easily by music than by any other means."(84)

The arsenal of audio-visual aids included, in addition to the use of the organs, the application of contemporary innovations such as the so called "magic lanterns" which could enlarge and project pictures and slides. Thus, in November 1895, one of the missionaries made a tour of the Razlog district

> with his magic lantern, meeting every point audiences which taxed the capacity of the largest buildings available. The gospel thus found entrance to the minds of no less than a thousand individuals within ten days.(85)

Several years later, the European Turkey Mission started to show stereoscopic views that gave the effect of three-dimensional images. In connection with this new practice, E. B. Haskell wrote with a certain amount of satisfaction that "the stereoscopic views are great wonder to the people. Someone is looking at them all the time."(86) The collection of the stereoscopic views that the missionaries had at their disposal included scenes from American life as well as views of American cities. It must have been a great attraction indeed for ordinary Bulgarians to see a "Chicago street with 14 story building" in 1901 when the stereoscopic views first became available to the European Turkey Mission.(87)

Less sensational aids in the missionary work of evangelizing were also put to good use. The Americans had great numbers of attractive cards with passages from the Bible printed on them. These proved to be very desirable to native children to whom they were distributed free of charge. This practice, for example, led to a great increase in Sunday School attendance by children in Samokov. In 1887, the station reported that often more than 200 people, including small children, began to attend the Sunday school because "a very large number of little children have been attracted by cards given them each Sabbath on wh/ich/ were printed the Golden Texts."(88) In addition to luring new listeners to the Protestants, the cards were also distributed throughout all evangelical communities in Southern Bulgaria with the likely purpose to reward the existing followers. The task of distribution was undertaken by two ladies among the American missionaries in the summer of 1889.(89)

In general, the missionaries were ready to use a wide variety of outside help if it could improve the effectiveness of their preaching. The newness and attractiveness of organs, the magic lanterns, the stereoscopic views, and the cards with Biblical texts were introduced and widely used in the struggle to reach more people, to open previously closed doors. At one point, the missionaries in the district of Philippopolis even gave medicine which quickly became a more powerful instrument of evangelizing than the most eloquent preaching. In the words of one of the missionaries, L. Bond: "for a little vegetable Pain Killer the most violent opposers now welcome our helper to their homes."(90) It was as if the missionaries were trading for access to Bulgarian homes, taking the old approach in dealing with children or with primitive tribes—"trinkets" for good will. Of course, the missionary approach was much more sophisticated, but the principle remained the same. The advantages given to them by their American background were certainly used to impress and to influence the native population in the desired direction.

The wide range of different approaches toward evangelizing the Bulgarians, the continuous work to create a well-organized and capable Protestant community, which in turn would influence the majority of the Bulgarian population, all produced results. The impressive attempt to change an entire people may be evaluated in many different manners. A numerical approach to that task, however, helps to present the general pictures of missionary accomplishment in Bulgaria.

4. *The Evangelization of Southern Bulgaria: A Statistical Evaluation*

The missionaries of the American Board sent to labor among the Bulgarians left a good number of pages documenting the statistical results of their efforts in all spheres, including the direct efforts to evangelize. Every year, the more traditional written reports from each station of the Board were accompanied by detailed Tabular Views which the missionaries sent to Boston as a numerical report of their work. In spite of gaps and periodic changes of forms to be filed by the missionaries, it is possible to produce a Table (Table 1) from the available data. The statistics left behind by the missionaries, however, are not completely reliable. The missionaries themselves repeatedly state that often there are inaccuracies and mistakes in data collected; yet, these are the only statistics available to us. In spite of possible errors, the available data provide a sufficient basis for objectivity evaluating the missionary activity of evangelizing. Since these figures were known to the missionaries, they will also aid us to better understand how the missionaries viewed their own work. The accepted point of view of American historians dealing with this subject is that the statistical record does not do justice to the missionary impact on Bulgaria. As W. W. Hall stated:

"The Protestant movement in Bulgaria has always been weakest in its statistical aspects."(91) Even if we take this judgement as truth, these results cannot be discarded as unimportant. They are one of the few substantive ways of understanding the actual measurable significance of the evangelizing work among the Bulgarians residing south of the Balkan Mountains. As a consequence of the conviction that the statistical results of the missionary activity are of little use in judging the success of the Americans, no statistical analysis of that activity exists.

Table 1 addresses this gap in the historical understanding of the Balkan missionary movement. The information contained in it pertains primarily to the 1880's, 1890's and the first decade of the twentieth century. In addition, data were found for 1870 and 1875. There is no summary information for 1897 and 1899; however, for 1899 the necessary data could be found in the separate station statistics. In 1898, the form to be filed was changed, a fact which explains why the number of out-stations and the number of places of preaching are combined as a single figure. In 1905, another form change occurred; therefore, data about the money supplied to the Mission by the American Board were no longer displayed. Such data were given only for the short period of 1899-1904 and for 1889. From 1890 to 1894 and in 1896 the figure entered under "Payments by the People" included the sum received from the sale of missionary and other publications which is given in explanatory notes. From 1908 on the Mission had one station which supervised work among Albanians. This is indicated by adding it to the number of the Bulgarian stations. All other figures for those years relate only to the Bulgarian work. Most of the sums of money were reported in piasters, except in 1870 and in 1884 when the amounts were entered in Turkish Liras. The Turkish Lira contained 100 piasters, and this rule was used to convert these amounts into piasters. The occasional empty spaces in the Table signify that the information was not available.

Analysis of the data shows that the most constant factor in forty years of missionary activity was the number of stations among the Bulgarians. From the start of the European Turkey Mission until 1894, four stations existed: Constantinople,

TABLE 1*

STATISTICAL RESULTS: EVANGELIZATION (1870-1909)

YEAR	STATIONS	OUT-STATIONS	MISSIONARIES ORDAINED**	NATIVES ORDAINED	PLACES OF PREACHING	AVERAGE CONGREGATION	# CHURCHES	# MEMBERS	NEW MEMBERS	PAYMENTS BY THE PEOPLE
1870	4	4	7; 3	7; 0	7	121	0	76		
1875	4	8	22; 10	21; 3	11	407	3	124	20	c. 5,800 ps.
1881[a]	4	15	23; 10	30; 3	18	973	4	188	29	7,704 ps.
1882[a]	4	14	24; 9	35; 2	22	1095	4	166	32	4,122 ps.
1883[a]	4	19	29; 11	36; 2	23	1256	5	294	22	59,202 ps.
1884[a]	4	19	24; 8	32; 3	15	1038	6	347	93	66,310 ps.
1885[a]	4	25	28; 10	38; 5	22	1381	7	404	58	75,860 ps.
1885[b]	4	24	26; 10	43; 5	26	1340	7	483	38	
1886	4	23	26; 10	62; 19	26	1457	8	553	68	76,446 ps.
1887	4	29	; 10	; 6	34	1607	8	650	113	79,738 ps.
1888	4	26	24; 10	77; 13	29	1682	8	682	98	142,737 ps.
1889	4	27	25; 10	55; 8	31	1885	9	729	82	103,031 ps.
1890	4	30	24; 10	71; 9	33	1844	12	827		176,639 ps.[c]
1891	4	33	27; 12	69; 7	38	1956	12		117	179,125 ps.[d]
1892	4	29	27; 12	70; 7	36	1995	13		67	156,000 ps.[e]
1893	4	36	27; 12	69; 9	39	2193	13		46	138,348 ps.[f]
1894	4	38	24; 11	78; 10	42	2278	14		49	171,948 ps.[g]
1895	5	44	23; 11	79; 12	47	2475	14	1008	79	158,656 ps.
1896	5	45	27; 12	80; 13	42	2423	14	1058	66	137,075.5 ps.

TABLE 1 cont.

YEAR	STATIONS	OUT-STATIONS	MISSIONARIES ORDAINED	NATIVES ORDAINED	PLACES OF PREACHING	AVERAGE CONGREGATION	# CHURCHES	# MEMBERS	NEW MEMBERS	PAYMENTS BY THE PEOPLE
1898	5	49	23; 10	80; 11		2606	16	1219	113	108,870 ps.
1899	5	58	22; 11	82; 14		2928		1270	73	112,746 ps.
1900	5	55	25; 10	93; 14		2887	16	1358	110	135,128 ps.
1901	4	56	28; 11	86; 16		2983	16	1415	77	118,531 ps.
1902	4	55	27; 11	94; 15		3277	16	1492	131	137,777 ps.
1903	4	56	28; 11	106; 16		3148	16	1435	44	129,542 ps.
1904	4	58	27; 11	94; 16		3184	16	1467	69	129,404 ps.
1905	4	58	28; 11	94; 17		3219	16	1523	87	114,327 ps.
1906	4	61	26; 10	99; 18		3283	17	1453	62	139,172 ps.
1907	4	60	26; 10	96; 15		3452	19	1408	67	142,564 ps.
1908	4+1	59	26; 10	108; 16		3254	19	1442	63	125,985 ps.
1909	4+1	56	26; 10	103; 17		3266	19	1456	94	164,100 ps.

*All the information compiled in Table 1 may be found in Tabular Views for the respective years in ABC 16.9, vols. 4, 7, 11, 14. The data for 1875 was taken from a Tabular View in the Clarke Papers.

**This column represents the # of missionaries, and # ordained (separated by ;). See, the next column, also.

[a]For year ending March 31.

[b]For April through December, 1885.

[c]72,569 piasters from sales of publications.

[d]57,931 piasters from sales of publications.

[e]51,914 piasters from sales of publications.

[f]41,372 piasters from sales of publications.

[g]58,119 piasters from sales of publications.

Monastir*, Philippopolis**, and Samokov. In 1894, a new station was added in the city of Salonica, a region of Macedonia within the Ottoman Empire. Five years later, however, the number of stations was again four after the European Turkey Mission ceased to administer the Constantinople Station. All the publishing work that had been done in Constantinople was transferred to Samokov in February 1898; and with the death in 1899 of Elias Riggs who had worked on a revision of a Bulgarian Bible Dictionary, the Constantinople Station no longer concerned itself with Bulgarian affairs.(92)

The fact that throughout the period the Mission did not increase its number of stations, however, does not indicate stagnation of its efforts since the number of outstations and places of regular worship did increase dramatically. By the end of the forty-year period, there was an increase of 800% which peaked in 1906 when there were 61 such locations. The increase in the number of missionaries was more modest but still quite respectable. From 1870 to 1909, that figure increased 3.7 times with the largest number of missionaries (29) in 1883. The increase was most dramatic from 1870-1875. During the rest of the time, the number of missionaries was always above twenty-two with an annual average of approximately twenty-five. In other works, following the peak in 1883, the number of missionaries remained quite constant. This constancy was especially impressive in terms of the number of ordained missionaries. There were usually ten during the entire period with minor variations, except in the initial year when there were only three.

* Monastir /present-day Bitola/ was occupied as a station in October 1873; see, J. W. Baird, "Annual Report of Monastir Station for the year ending June 18th 1874," ABC 16.9, v. 5.

** Philippopolis was relinquished as a station from October 1871, to October 1878. The missionary force was removed to Eski Zagra. When the station was reoccupied, Eski Zagra was permanently abandoned as a station; see Henry C. Haskell, "12th Annual Report of the Philippopolis Station: 1870-1871," Clarke Papers; L. Bond, "Annual Report of Philippopolis Station for 1878-79," Clarke Papers.

Adrianople, which was one of the founding stations of the European Turkey Mission, was no longer a station in the period represented in Table 1. The last annual report from Adrianople is dated 1868; see J. N. Ball, "Report of the Adrianople Station," ABC 16.9, v. 5.

In contrast to the steady number of Americans was the growth in number of natives aiding the missionaries. Throughout the forty years under consideration, the number of Bulgarians increased almost 15 times with an even greater growth in the number of ordained men (the starting point of comparison is zero). The figure given for 1886 (19) is obviously a mistake since both in the preceding and the subsequent years the figures are considerably less. It should be noted that until 1895 there were usually (except in 1886 and in 1888) more ordained missionaries than ordained Bulgarians. Clearly the process of educating and training native leadership developed slowly and without remarkable success.

The most dynamic growth in the European Turkey Mission was in regard to the number of Protestant churches, of members of the church, and of people that comprised the congregation. The figures indicating the number of churches show uninterrupted growth, starting from zero and reaching 19. Similarly, the increase in the number of church members is 19.1 times greater in 1909 than in 1870, with an annual average gain in church membership of almost 49. Recognizing that in terms of percentages the growth in this area was quite spectacular, it was minor in reality compared with the vast population that was still unconverted. According to missionary data at the end of the period, in 1909 they were laboring among 4,551,000 people.(93) At this same time, the missionaries could report only 1,456 church members. Obviously, the future of Protestantism in Southern Bulgaria was less than promising.

The data regarding average church congregations are a bit more impressive from the missionary point of view but they still do not significantly improve the overall impression of American efforts to reform the Bulgarians. The number of people that attended Protestant churches increased 27 times, but in 1909 the total number was only 3,266. Once more, there was a significant relative statistical increase but minuscule impact in real terms. These modest results explain the fact that the missionaries could not and did not see the creation of separate Protestant religious communities as a goal in themselves. They also explain the willingness of the Americans to try a wide variety of methods in their desire to reach and influence a greater number of Bulgarians.

Clearly, the missionaries were able to assemble only a rather small group of followers. But were the native converts a reliable force? One good indicator is certainly the ability and willingness of the Bulgarian Protestants to financially support the cause. If we consider the overall increase in payments by the natives, the result closely parallels the increase in the average congregation size. While the number of people attending Protestant churches increased 27 times, the contributions by these same people increased approximately 28.3 times*. If an attempt is made to calculate the average contribution per person by using the numbers given for the average congregation, the outcome is not easy to classify. There are great variations: from 3.76 piasters per person in 1882 to 64.1 piasters per person in 1895. Whether these contributions were sufficient may be considered in terms of the realization that the recommended monthly salary for unmarried preachers in villages in the 1880s was 400 piasters.(94) That native contributions were obviously deficient is illustrated even more clearly when we consider the ratio between the payments made by the people and those made by the American Board.** Based on the availability of sufficient data, such a comparison can be made only for six years: 1889, and 1899 to 1903. The ratio for 1889 is 1:2.5, for 1899, 1:2.02, for 1900, 1:1.9, for 1901, 1:2.17, for 1902, 1:2.09, and for 1903, 1:2.05. As a rule, the American Board had to contribute at least twice as much as the amount collected from Bulgarian Protestants. From a financial point of view, the missionaries might even be considered fortunate in

* No attempt was made to determine the changing monetary value of the piaster and its effect on the contributions. The missionaries did not make any adjustments and it was impossible to find enough information to calculate the real value of the collected sums of money throughout the period. Occasionally, evidence pointed to the changing value of the piaster; however, such instances were too rare. See, for example, J. H. House, "Short Report of the Colportage Work of Salonica Stsation for 1898," ABC 16.9, v. 10; J. H. House, "Report of Salonica Station of the European Turkey Mission from July 7, 1899 to May 2, 1900," Clarke Papers.

An assumption is made that the amounts given for the years following 1896 did not include publication sales. For the years when the figures include sales from publications, the calculation is done excluding these sales.

** The missionaries of the European Turkey Mission had the American Board as their major financial source; however, they received more or less regular payments from organizations such as the American Bible society, the American Tract Society, etc.

their lack of success among the Bulgarians. A larger following might have meant more native financial input but also a need for more paid workers, more buildings, etc. Given the existing rate of native contributions, a larger Protestant following might possibly have meant a larger expenditure for the American Board.

The most obvious conclusion that can be drawn from the assembled information is that the missionary involvement of the American Board among the Bulgarians showed steady but very slow growth. Still, the Americans, in spite of the discouraging statistics, did not leave—a fact which is not surprising considering the great faith and perseverance that they manifested in their deeds and writings.

5. *Missionaries about the Missionary Effort*

The Americans labored among the Bulgarians with definite ideas and opinions about the importance and significance of their work. They understood the exact results of their efforts in terms of figures, and they did not ignore these results. They were also able, through long years of experience, to develop additional insights relating to the effect of their evangelizing work, insights which the language of numbers could not always explain.

Often the missionaries would measure the results of their work by pointing out rather abstract or behavioral changes in the Bulgarians since their arrival. A statement made in 1884 by one of the missionaries, W. E. Locke, is a good example of such an approach. For him, the evidence that "God's truth is marching" in their field was the following observation: "Little by little ideas of freedom and liberty and justice are spreading."(95) Applying similar criteria, Rev. J. F. Clarke remarked in 1888: "It seems to me that the Mission work in Bulgaria has already been of great benefit to the whole nation—lifting them above the Servians* in many

* The missionaries always kept the vision of their work in world perspective. They were hoping that when their task was completed in Bulgaria, the Bulgarians would play an important role in the conversion of neighboring nations and the Slavs in general. For example, in 1885, one of the better known Bulgarian followers of the American Board would express this feeling in writing about the Bulgarian Evangelical Society: "We hope and pray that the day will soon come when the Society. . .will be a great power in the Balkan Peninsula." One of the missionaries had an even bolder expectation for the

respects."(96) Clearly, the missionaries were inclined to think in terms of the entire Bulgarian nation when they deliberated on the effect of their evangelical work. This vision certainly corresponds to their unchanging desire to see all Bulgarians reformed, to influence the entire nation.

In other less abstract observations, the missionaries simply noted that the natives who had embraced Protestantism seem to become better human beings. Following a tour in the town of Monastir, one of the missionary wives wrote that there was a great change in the women who became Protestants. According to Mrs. R. R. Bond: "All have learned to read a little. . .Their homes are much neater and in their personal appearance there is a marked change."(97) Such transformations, even though not directly related to spiritual matters, were most welcome by the missionaries since they were the best advertisement for the Protestant cause. The potential beneficial influence of the converted natives on their fellow Bulgarians is indicated by an anonymous missionary when describing Protestants in Bansko. At gatherings for meals during fairs "if there are Protestants present the whole company wait for them to ask God's blessing before eating, and the presence of a few Protestants causes the company not to call for wine, or only for a small quantity."(98) Such changes had more to do with morality than with spirituality, but still the missionaries obviously considered them important results. In addition, observations like these provided more encouragement for the Americans who knew that the work of evangelization was not proceeding in the way they had hoped. The tendency to replace religious criteria with others in evaluating the results to evangelize directly was to a certain degree due to the realization that other, not strictly evangelical, aspects of the missionary enterprise were more welcome and were therefore sometimes expanding at the expense of the former.* A statement by G. D. Marsh, one of

Bulgarians. In 1891, H. C. Haskell wrote in a letter to his son and Bulgarian missionary, Edward: "As to the 'future' of the Bulgns—I think they may be of invaluable service in Xtinizing *Russia*" /Haskell's emphasis/.

See respectively, J. J. Sitchaneff,, "Bulgarian Evangelical Society," *Missionary News from Bulgaria* 2:2; and H. C. Haskell to E. B. Haskell, February 11, 1891, Haskell Papers.

* This problem will be discussed at length in later chapters.

the missionaries who was stationed in Philippopolis, indicates that the missionaries understood that evangelization was not always the most important feature of their activity. The Philippopolis Station was not involved in educational or publishing work; commenting on this fact, one of the 'brethren'* told Marsh: "I rejoice in the work you are doing in your station. Your work is evangelizing, the work of most of us is only civilizing."(99)

When the missionaries considered the religious aspects of their effort to gain Protestant converts, they displayed a great amount of realism in evaluating the impact they had made. Marsh, for example, commented that a "demand for preaching. . .is. . .a direct result of our evangelistic efforts in Bulgaria."(100) This was one of the few concrete outcomes that was strictly religious in nature. Another one of the Americans, H. C. Haskell, while contemplating the result of twenty-two years of his personal involvement with the Bulgarians, concluded that "the growth of this /the missionary/ work from 1865 to 1893, tho. far less than we have desired must yet be to. . .us, a solid gratification."(101) He did not explain the reasons for his gratification in detail, but it is clear that the missionaries did not overestimate the impact of their activity, and even though aware of the modest results, they were proud of their work.

Haskell's son, Edward, left another even less joyous opinion of the effectiveness of the missionary work. In a personal letter, dated January 1900, he wrote: "If the work goes forward in one part of the field it goes backward in another, and so we swing around the circle!"(102) Most likely this reflection was the product of a momentary mood of uncertainty and despair, but it was still an important piece of evidence about the lack of illusions among the missionaries. The realization that success was nowhere in the foreseeable future made the Americans even more determined to pursue their work. In other words, the faith that the missionaries must have possessed did not blind them to the general ineffectiveness of the work in their field. They fully understood what was lacking in the European Turkey Mission, but by a wonderful ability to persevere they did not relinquish what they thought was their obligation to

* It was not clear here whether Marsh meant an American or a Bulgarian.

the Bulgarians. One of the best examples illustrating this type of reasoning among the missionaries comes from the annual report of the Philippopolis Station for 1906-1907:

> One percent of 5,000.000 /this was the approximate figure for the Bulgarians in missionary documents/ is 50,000. Does any such number, or one half of it even show any sign of seeking the Lord...and this after the circulation of many ten thousands of the New Testament among them for forty years? There can be no question that they do not. The need then of our work among them, has been *as great as the need of their salvation* /underscored in the original/.(103)

Another frank admission of the remoteness of achieving the final missionary goal came in 1908 during the official celebration of the fiftieth anniversary of missionary work among the Bulgarians. On this important occasion, Rev. Robert Thomson summed up the expectations of his colleagues:

> In anticipating the future it was felt that Bulgaria would probably never become in name Protestant or model its Christianity exactly after the Western type. But the belief was no less decidedly expressed that the nation would be truly evangelized.(104)

A certain dichotomy was thus present in the missionary thinking. The Americans definitely acknowledged the meager results of their efforts and the bleak future that awaited them in this respect, but they stubbornly adhered to the original goal of the European Turkey Mission. The only glimmers of hope which they could see were not in the sphere of evangelizing but in the character of the Bulgarian people. In evaluating the religious aspect of their influence among the Bulgarians, the missionaries could point to only a few influences which did not strictly belong to the religious field. Edward B. Haskell wrote an article for one of the American missionary publications in which he analyzed the American evangelizing efforts:

> The Bulgars have proved the most responsive to American Christian influence of any Balkan people.

> Yet it would be presumptuous to claim that all their progress is due to it. It has had some share, however, in producing the following results:
>
> 1. A religious tolerance unapproached elsewhere in the Levant.
>
> 2. The temperance cause has made great progress in Bulgaria.
>
> 3. The great advance of socialism in Bulgaria shows an interest in human welfare, an idealism and a spirit of brotherhood which are essentially Christian virtues.(105)

All the results cited are highly questionable. For the purposes of the present chapter, however, it is enough to emphasize once again that the missionaries did not view their evangelizing efforts as successful. They were, though, able to point out certain features of contemporary Bulgarian life which they felt resulted from their efforts. In this case, it was religious tolerance; in earlier writings, it was a demand for preaching among the Bulgarians. These are essentially the only religious consequences of the American involvement, in addition to a small number of converts. Other changes that the missionaries might claim were essentially non-religious. This certainly indicates that the Americans possessed quite a broad vision of their task in Bulgaria. Of course, they would have been much happier with great evangelizing success. However, they maintained a sharp awareness of reality and were certainly willing to advertise their achievements in other than missionary fields. At times, they even blurred the distinction between the evangelizing mission and the "civilizing" essence of their work. Certainly the missionaries did not come to Bulgaria only to see women become neater housewives and men limit their consumption of wine. Even such simple changes, however, were important for them — and not only because the religious impact upon the Bulgarians was so minor; possibly the Americans truly cared about the Bulgarians.

6. *The Evangelizing Effort and the Bulgarians*

The missionaries nurtured no illusions about their own record in European Turkey. They also made a continuous effort to analyze the effectiveness of their Bulgarian helpers. In so doing, the Americans tended to comment more frequently on the problems they had in their joint work with the Bulgarian Protestants than on the positive elements. Perhaps this reflected the actual state of things in the Mission; perhaps this was a part of the psychology of the missionary. At least in one respect, however, American criticisms did correspond to a well documented fact—that only a small number of Bulgarian followers could act as preachers or pastors. The figures in Table 1 clearly illustrate this point; during the last three years represented (1906-1909), for example, the number of churches was greater than the number of ordained natives. This tendency was clear by the late 1880's.

The missionaries themselves complained about the situation on many occasions. In 1885, for instance, the Samokov Protestant community could not maintain its own preacher but used the free service of one of the missionaries. One of the secretaries of the American Board in Boston wrote in indignation regarding this fact: "There is no propriety in our sending out missionaries to be pastors of Bulgarian churches."(106) The same inability of the Bulgarians to maintain their own preachers and pastors was also present in Monastir and Philippopolis. One of the Americans in Monastir, J. W. Baird, complained about this unfortunate circumstance in the following way:

> The native brethren when urged and pressed to do more meet pressure by passive resistance. They...reduce us to the alternative of (1) either preaching ourselves or having no Protestant preaching in the city. (107)

In Philippopolis, the same problem existed, clearly stemming from financial considerations. The men educated by the Americans to become preachers or pastors in the Samokov missionary school "want to go back to Samokove* as teachers or into the army as officers." These Bulgarians indicated that they "cannot live on the salary offered by the people which the latter say they think is enough."(108) The sensitive topic of salaries for the native helpers was often a point of friction

* This is often how the missionaries transcribed the name of Samokov.

between Americans and Bulgarians. The policy of the European Turkey Mission, which followed guidelines established by the American Board, was clearly stated at the second annual meeting of the Mission. The missionaries found it best "to give as little aid as possible and not enfeeble the persons aided. The maximum being 1/2 of the amount needed for the object."(109) This rule was generally applied not only in terms of salaries but in all other cases, such as the building of churches, etc. Obviously, the other half had to be supplied by the native congregations, and their ability to provide the necessary finances became critically important.

The list of salaries decided upon in 1881 ranged from 4 to 10 Turkish Liras monthly for preachers.(110) During that time a teacher in the missionary school for girls in Monastir received 25 Turkish Liras yearly in addition to free board. A teacher in the Bulgarian school for girls in the same town received the significantly higher salary of 120 Turkish Liras and free board.(111) This example illustrates the great disparity in the salaries of educated Bulgarians paid by the government and of educated Bulgarians serving the Protestant community. The latter were definitely disadvantaged financially and, more importantly, they knew this and constantly complained about the lack of means. References to that effect were quite numerous in missionary correspondence. In 1879, for example, G. D. Marsh wrote to Boston that "some of the helpers have expressed themselves as quite dissatisfied with the rates we supply."(112) A few years later, it became clear that, in fact, "one of the main efforts of the native brethren. . .was to raise the salaries of preachers."(113) Some of the missionaries were so overwhelmed by constant complaints that they showed signs of irritability when the problem was discussed. Thus, the only medical doctor of the European Turkey Mission, F. L. Kingsbury, wrote in 1895 that "our native brethren are quite constantly saying to us that the evangelical work is threatened with disaster because salaries of native agents are so small." He even proceeded to comment; "There are many critical things. . .that I might say of our native friends with reference to their love for money."(114) Not all missionaries sought the reasons for the continuous demand for higher salaries in the character of the native Protestants. Some Americans looked at their own financial condition and concluded that the grievances of the Bulgarian workers were quite legitimate. In 1907, for example, L. F. Ostrander, who was residing in Samokov, compared his own income to that of the Bulgarian pastors:

> When we (Mrs. Ostrander and myself), without children. . .were able out of a salary of $800 a year to lay by only the $42 which we put annually into life insurance. . .the wonder to me is how our pastors, with families of two, three, four or five children manage to get along at all on salaries of $265 or $315.(115)

The significant discrepancy between the payment of missionaries and that of native helpers sometimes contributed to the creation of strained relations between American and Bulgarian Protestants*. On at least two occasions, representatives of the Bulgarian preachers officially approached the missionaries in order to voice their unhappiness about the relatively low rate of salaries for native helpers. In 1902, the Bulgarians attempted to present this concern in relation to the success of the general missionary work. In their words, "the policy of the mission in paying so scanty salaries to the native workers has been to a large extent detrimental to the work itself." To them the large salaries for missionaries could easily be converted into smaller salaries for more native helpers since "there should be fewer foreigners and more natives on the field."(119) A few years later, the same grievance was voiced, this time to explain the lack of preachers in the field. In a letter dated August 30, 1904, to the European Turkey Mission, the Bulgarian preachers recommended that the material support for native workers should be increased so

* The funds that the American Board allotted to the missionaries represented as a rule the largest portion of the annual contributions for the European Turkey Mission. Most often the ratio between the amount for missionary salaries and the amount designated for the so called "general work", which included salaries for native workers, money for publication, etc., was roughly 1:1, with a strong tendency for the former to exceed all other expenses.(116) When the American Board was in difficult financial straits, cuts in expenditures were made so as to affect missionary salaries the least. In 1896, for instance, when severe cuts were made in appropriations for most of the missions of the Board, there was a 42% cut in the amount for general work and only 10% was cut for missionary salaries.(117) Clearly, the missionaries were the first priority of the American Board. As G. D. Marsh expressed it: "There is always enough money for missionaries, however much we are pinched, or the work is cut down."(118)

that "new workers would prefer preaching to other occupations."(120)

This type of reasoning among the native helpers certainly had foundations, and, in fact, the missionaries themselves would use very similar arguments when attempting to acquire more financial means from Boston. In 1896, much earlier than the above complaints, the annual report of Monastir Station contained the following warning:

> If we are to attempt any longer to live 'at this poor dying rate'* it behooves the mission and the Board to ask themselves whether they are wise in maintaining two missionaries but on average only about 1½ helpers, and whether they are not treating those missionaries unjustly by asking them to work without tools.(121)

The low salaries for native workers and the lack of preachers in the field were actually two aspects of one problem—the inability of the Bulgarian Protestants, due to their small numbers in addition to all other possible reasons, to support their religious community financially. Given the policy of the American Board to provide only moderate aid to the native workers, there was no real hope for great change. The missionaries would constantly talk and write about the need of self-support in European Turkey and constantly they would conclude that this goal seemed out of reach for the foreseeable future. By 1909, there were only two self-supporting churches. The first one to briefly become self-supporting was the church in Bansko during the late 1890's. In the next decade, the mission could report only two such churches—one in Philippopolis from 1908 and, the following year, one in Sofia.(122)

The missionaries tried different means to collect money. In 1874, the members of the newly founded church in the city of Iambol adopted "tithe giving"; during the second half of the 1880's "the envelope system of giving" gradually became the accepted method (123)—but still no decisive improvement would be reported in the direction of self-help. The native

* The same year, the missionaries were faced with unprecedented cuts in financial support from the American Board.

Protestants not only could not gather enough to pay their pastors, but they also relied on sources other than the American Board when circumstances could not offer any other possibility. In 1887, for example, the missionaries were forced to approve the raising of about 150 Turkish Liras in Europe and England for the purpose of building a church in Sofia.(124) Two decades later, the pastor of the same church was sent to Germany, England, and the United States to search for more help, this time for needed repairs of the church building. This was again done "with the reluctant consent" of the missionaries.(125) These events, however, pale in comparison with an almost scandalous development in the early 1900's when it became clear that one of the Bulgarian pastors was appealing regularly to his former theological classmates in the United States for funds to cover his living expenses.(126) Such occurrences were only an exception, but they spoke loudly about the hopelessness of any quick development of self-support among the natives.

The missionaries had a clear understanding of this situation, and during one particularly critical time, in 1896, they even contemplated a drastic reduction in the missionary staff as a means to force the Bulgarians into self-support. As one of the Americans wrote, "as long as so many missionaries are here" the natives will feel "that the Board must have money."(127) The belief was that if only half of the existing missionary force remained, then possibly the Bulgarian Protestants would start to be more self-reliant. These plans never became a reality. However, their very existence indicates the mistrust and at times even desperation expressed by the missionaries where questions of native self-support were concerned.

The failure of the Bulgarian Protestants to supply the needed number of preachers, to support these preachers, and, in general, to become self-reliant even after more than half a century of missionary involvement probably influenced the overall attitude that the Americans formed toward their helpers. Immediately, it should be noted that the criteria the Americans applied cannot always be regarded as reasonable. Such was the case of an opinion expressed by Robert Thomson who wrote in 1884 regarding a conference with the native helpers: "I was very thankful to find how...the views and judgements of our native helpers more and more nearly approximate to, and finally completely coincide with, those which we bring them from the west."(128) Pronouncements like this undoubtedly project feelings of superiority—not in terms of a religious nature which might be expected but in terms of a supposed inherent advantage in being "from the West." It seems that Thomson expected the Bulgarian Protestants to conform to some "Western" way of thinking in order to be good helpers in the missionary enterprise. It is difficult to determine whether other missionaries subscribed exactly to Thomson's views. However, as will be shown in Chapter IV, the Americans tended to see themselves and their ways as representing not just Protestantism but the West, in general, as superior to the natives. Feelings such as these aid in explaining why missionaries often distrusted their native helpers.

This aspect of the American treatment of Bulgarian Protestants is most clearly illustrated by the missionary reluctance to accept native input in the actual management of Mission affairs. The regular conferences, starting in the early 1890s, were more consultative meetings where the opinion of the natives might be expressed. The actual decision-making was done at the annual meetings of the European Turkey Mission and also, for day-to-day matters, at the station level. The Americans were quite reluctant as a group to welcome not only real Bulgarian participation at such occasions but also Bulgarian opinions. In 1875, T. L. Byington, the future editor of the missionary newspaper, openly criticized his colleagues for their lack of sensitivity to native opinion. In a letter dated June 26, he wrote:

> I put myself in the place of an intelligent Bulgarian pastor and ask myself whether I have patience enough and grace enough to continue to cooperate in a common work with those excluding me from all participation in their councils.(129)

Surely, this very comment was a credit to its author; however, the fact remained that the missionaries were slow in accepting Bulgarian Protestants as equals in the affairs of the Mission.

The first steps in the direction of joint work were taken in the early 1880's. At the eleventh annual meeting of the Mission in the spring of 1880, the Americans discussed at length the role that the native workers should play and decided that the time had not yet come to involve them in decision-making. More specifically, they thought that Bulgarians should be consulted regarding the location of pastors and helpers but that they could not decide these questions.(130) These decisions were reversed, to a certain extent, at the following annual meeting in 1881 when the Americans invited representatives of the Bulgarian Evangelical Society to act as school board members, as members of the Publication Committee, and as members of the committee for annual school examinations. In addition, the same society was invited "to send every year three delegates to attend as Corresponding members the open sessions of the Annual Meetings" of the Mission.(131) Certainly, a departure from the earlier missionary policy was initiated, and in 1883, the native Protestants were received as full and voting members of the conference which met in Samokov and was the first general conference of workers from the entire field.(132)

The other important step in overcoming missionary reluctance to accept their native workers as equals in decision-making was taken in 1890 at the nineteenth annual meeting of the Mission. Adopting a policy which Boston strongly advocated, the missionaries voted to "heartily endorse the principle. . .that the general work of the schools and stations be carried on. . .by the joint action of Bulgarian and American workers.(133) There are indications that this principle was indeed applied in the actual missionary work, with Samokov station as the pioneer. During the same year, the Protestants in this city formed a joint committee, consisting of three Americans, but only two Bulgarians*, which directed all evangelistic work.(134) Again, trust regarding the natives was not complete, as the Americans, who retained more representatives than the Bulgarians, remained dominant.

The interpretation of the principle of "joint" action was rather narrow since toward the end of the first decade of the

* One of the documents indicated that there were three members each from the two nationalities, but it had an earlier date than the one giving the above figures. Given the missionary tradition in this respect, an assumption was made that the actual figure for Bulgarian members was two. See J. F. Clarke, "Report of Samokov Station 1891-2," ABC 16.9, v. 10 and references in endnote 141.

20th century, the Americans decided that certain positions were not suitable for the natives, after all. In 1906, the European Turkey Mission declared at its consecutive annual meeting that with regard to the Samokov Station "it would be unwise to put the station treasury into the hands of any native, since this would let him into the private affairs of each missionary and native co-worker."(135) Mistrust and even ideas of missionary superiority can only explain such a position. It should be emphasized that Samokov was the most progressive station in terms of fully accepting the native workers. But even there complete trust was not evident. At other stations, such as Salonica, it took much longer to establish even the practice of joint committees. There, the missionaries attempted as late as 1910, or twenty years after the principle was adopted, "the experiment of working with an advisory committee."(136)

American caution regarding the involvement of the Bulgarian Protestants in certain spheres of missionary activity is hardly surprising. The native followers failed to satisfy missionary requirements in terms of both financial contributions and the production of a sufficient number of preachers. These were serious grievances which surely influenced the American decision concerning the exact role of the Bulgarians. A feeling or an understanding of the American "right of superior direction" pervaded the American missionaries' attitude. The very phrase, in fact, was used in correspondence between Americans regarding the work of the Bulgarian Evangelical Society mentioned above.(137) Such an interpretation of the attitudes displayed by the missionaries might also be supported by instances of direct criticism toward the native workers. Kingsbury's remarks noted above regarding the Bulgarian "love for money" is such an example. H. C. Haskell, also spoke at least twice in his private correspondence about disappointing features of the Bulgarian helpers. Once he described them as "poor in goods and ability,"(138) and on another occasion ascribed negative characteristics to the entire native preaching force:

> The preachers—3 probably of too small caliber,—one or two not very well fitted spiritually,—one good one in feeble health,—another, an uneasy, changing man;

another has an Am. wife and can't live on any salary he can get; another would like to take ten or more mos. for touring. . .(138)

There is no reason to doubt the honesty of Haskell's depressing commentary on the abilities and qualities of the Bulgarian preachers. Clearly, if some of the missionaries would express such opinions, they would also not be willing to accept the native workers as equal partners. Only one of the documents gives a positive view of Bulgarian Protestant preachers. It relates not to their moral and spiritual qualities but rather to their education. In the words of a missionary from the Monastir Station: "Compared to their audiences the preachers educated in Samokov are better educated than Cong'l preachers in America compared with their hearers."(140) Even this good feature of the Bulgarians, however, was something attributed to missionary training and not so much as a result of native efforts.

The missionary view of their Bulgarian followers generally was critical and serves as further evidence of the overall lack of notable success in evangelizing the natives. The statistical data and the evaluation of the missionaries themselves all point to the same result. One final question is how the Bulgarians, either Protestant or Orthodox, evaluated the European Turkey Mission.

The Bulgarians, as a rule, did not regard as most important the purely religious, or evangelical, aspect of the American Board's mission. Protestants and Orthodox alike wrote about other features of the missionary effort—mainly its educational and literary activities. In the few cases when evangelical work was discussed in itself, opinion was divided. The Bulgarian Protestants typically would speak of the "regenerative" role of the Americans without giving much detail.(141) No negative accounts by persons sympathetic to the missionaries who might actually analyze the efforts for conversion to Protestantism seem to exist. Such authors merely note that there were evangelical efforts and they understood them to be a good thing. The Bulgarian followers of the European Turkey Mission did not even attempt to approach the evangelizing effort objectively. Obviously, they were not likely to question their mentors in any way.

A slightly greater variety of opinion was voiced among non-Protestant Bulgarians of that time. Predictably, some would view the efforts for conversion by the Americans in very negative terms. One of the greatest Bulgarian leaders from the period of National Revival, Li͡uben Karavelov, wrote that the missionary work spread delusions.(142) Other opponents of Protestantism acknowledged some real American Protestant impact. A. Shopov, for example, viewed the effects of Protestant propaganda as partially successful among the Bulgarian intelligentsia. Of course, he considered such successes a very unfortunate development.(143)

In general, Bulgarians who feared the "dangers" of American missionary involvement in European Turkey opposed evangelizing efforts for patriotic reasons. One of the best expressions of Bulgarian concerns came from the pages of *Makedonii͡a*, the newspaper edited by another famous literary figure in Bulgarian history, Petko R. Slaveikov. In the early 1870's, the paper summarized in the following manner the feelings of most opponents of Protestantism:

> We are against the Protestants with all the cruelty of a person who feels all the bad consequences of the division of the people due to such religious wrangles.(144)

Comments like this do not really evaluate the evangelizing efforts of the missionaries, but they are the typical of the Bulgarian response to the entire issue.

The American missionaries did, however, have a real impact on church life in Bulgaria. The structuring of the reestablished Bulgarian Exarchate was accomplished in such a manner that several principles, typical of Protestantism, were incorporated. For example, the rule of the removability of the Exarch, lay participation in church government, and other ideas characteristic of Protestant church practice became a part of Orthodoxy in Bulgaria. As established by Bulgarian scholars, these were the concrete results of the Mission's effort to reform the Bulgarian population.(145) Curiously, the Americans did not claim this feature of their contribution in the direction of religious change among the natives. Nevertheless, the partial adoption of the Protestant model in church government in Bulgaria constitutes an important aspect of the missionary presence in the country.

List of References

1. Nikolai Genchev, *Bŭlgarsko vŭzrazhdane*, (Sofia, 1978), p. 8.

2. *Kratka istoriia na Bŭlgariia*, (Sofia, 1983), p. 154. This work contains a short but thorough presentation of the history of the Bulgarian Revival as seen by present-day Bulgarian historians. See, pp. 154-210.

3. Clarke, *Bible Societies*.

4. Ibid., pp. 142-143.

5. Hall, p. 15.

6. "Extracts from the Journal of Mr. Dwight, in Roomelia," *Missionary Herald* 31 (1835): 169-172.

7. Cited in Hall, p. 15.

8. Clarke, *Bible Societies*, p. 280.

9. Ibid.

10. Ibid., p. 282.

11. Elias Riggs, *Reminiscences for My Children*, (n.p., 1891), p. 11.

12. Clarke, *Bible Societies*, p. 132.

13. Hall, p. 13.

14. Mojzes, p. 57.

15. Cyrus Hamlin, *Among the Turks*, (New York: Robert Carter and Brothers, 530 Broadway, 1878), p. 262.

16. Ibid.

17. Cyrus Hamlin, *My Life and Times*, 2nd ed., (Boston and Chicago: Congregational Sunday School Publishing Society, 1893), p. 387.

18. Ibid.

19. Hamlin, *Among the Turks*, p. 272.

20. C. F. Morse, "Annual Report of Adrianople Station, Adrianople, May 30th 1859", Clarke Papers.

21. J. F. Clarke to Dr. Anderson, June 8, 1865, Papers of the American Board of Commissioners for Foreign Missions, hereafter ABC, 16.9, vol. 4.

22. James F. Clarke, "Protestantism and the Bulgarian Church Question in 1861," *Essays in the History of Modern Europe*, Donald C. McKay, ed., (Freeport, New York: Books for Libraries Press, Inc., 1968), pp. 89-90.

23. William W. Meriam, "3rd Annual Report of the Philippopolis Station," Clarke Papers.

24. A. S. T͡sanov, "Istorii͡ata na Bŭlgarskoto Evangelsko Blagotvoritelno D-vo," *I͡ubileina kniga na Bŭlgarskoto Evangelsko Blagotvoritelno Druzhestvo po sluchai petdesetgodishninata mu 1875-1925*, (Sofia, 1925), p. 8.

25. J. F. Clarke, "Journal of Tour by J. F. Clarke accompanied by Evancho Tondjorov Nov. 25-Dec. 16, 1864," Clarke Papers.

26. For a detailed description of the events see James F. Clarke, "Protestantism."

27. Henry C. Haskell, "11th Annual Report of the Philippopolis Station 1869-1870, Philippopolis May 5th, 1870", Clarke Papers.

28. "Mission to European Turkey," *Missionary Herald* 66/12 (December, 1870): 389.

29. Mojzes, p. 623.

30. "Mission to European Turkey", p. 388.

31. T. Ikonomov, *Protestantskata propaganda u nas i neinite polzi za Bulgarii͡a*, 3rd ed., (Shumen, 1892), p. 29.

32. Albert L. Long, "Convention of Bulgarian Missionaries. Eski Zaghra May 6, 1863," Clarke Papers, and Henry C. Haskell, "Records of a Convention of Bulgarian Missionaries held at Philippopolis, March 8th-14th 1866," ABC 16.9, vol. 4.

33. J. F. Clarke to Dr. Anderson, June 8, 1865, ABC 16.9, vol. 4.

34. See the first annual reports of those stations in ABC 16.9, vol. 4.

35. Nikola Ganchev Enicherev, *Vŭzpominanii͡a i belezhki*, (Sofia, 1906), p. 53.

36. Chas F. Morse, "The First Annual Report of the Sofia Station 1863," ABC 16.9, vol. 4.

37. Petŭr Dinekov, *Sofia prez XIX vek do Osvobozhdenieto na Bulgarii͡a*, (Sofia, 1937), p. 154.

38. Henry C. Haskell, "Journal of a Tour N. W. of Phil. by Henry C. Haskell, March 4th-30th 1864," Clarke Papers.

39. Stoi͡anov, "Nachalo", p. 55.

40. T. L. Byington, "The Third Annual Report of the Eski Zagra Station", ABC 16.9, vol. 4.

41. "Minutes of the Convention of the Missionaries to the

Bulgarians, held at Philippopolis, March 1869", ABC 16.9, vol. 4.

42. I. F. Pettibone, "Minutes of the 30th Annual Meeting of the W. Turkey Mission", Clarke Papers.

43. H. P. Page, "Report of Samokov Station 1871-1872", ABC 16.9, vol. 5; J. F. C. 63/1, p. 21, Clarke Papers.

44. See the Annual Tabular View for 1894 in ABC 16.9, vol. 11.

45. *Missionary News from Bulgaria* 47:6.

46. /H. C. Haskell/, "Visit to Prilep", Haskell Papers.

47. J. F. Clarke to N. G. Clarke (sic), Apr. 30, 1881, ABC 16.9, vol. 8.

48. Ibid.

49. James L. Barton to L. F. Ostrander, July 27, 1906, Clarke Papers.

50. Ibid.

51. Cited in Hall, pp. 203-204.

52. Ibid., p. 204.

53. See Annual Tabular Views for 1908 and 1909 in ABC 16.9, vol. 15.

54. J. F. C. 64/1, p. 27, Clarke Papers.

55. E. W. Jenney to N. G. Clark, May 4, 1880, ABC 16.9, vol. 5; for the actual resolution see J. F. C. 64/2, p. 117, Clarke Papers.

56. W. E. Locke, "Annual Report of Samokove Station 1881 and 2", ABC 16.9, vol. 7.

57. J. Henry House, "Report of Samokove Station for the year 1882-1883", ABC 16.9, vol. 7.

58. Cited in Hall, p. 69.

59. "Conference of Churches", *Missionary News from Bulgaria* 18:4.

60. Geo. D. Marsh, "Annual Report of the Philippopolis Station for the year ending Apr. 15th 18898", ABC 16.9, vol. 7.

61. *Zornit͡sa* (Plovdiv), October 29, 1909, p. 3.

62. "Conferences", *Missionary News from Bulgaria* 33:1.

63. Ibid.

64. Ibid.

65. E. M. Stone, "Church Conference in Bulgaria", *Missionary News from Bulgaria* 25:4.

66. Ibid.

67. "Conferences", *Missionary News from Bulgaria* 38:6-7; "Church Conferences", *Missionary News from Bulgaria* 44:2.

68. J. F. Clarke, "Annual Report of Samokov Station, for 1892-3", ABC 16.9, vol. 10; "Meetings in Bulgaria", *Missionary News from Bulgaria* 44:2.

69. "Conferences", *Missionary News from Bulgaria* 33:1.

70. For example, see /E. M. Stone/ "A New Church and Pastor," *Missionary News from Bulgaria* 50:4 *Zornit͡sa* (T͡sarigrad /Istanbul/), November 16, 1896, p. 177; *Zornit͡sa* (Plovdiv), October 29, 1909, p. 3.

71. E. M. Stone, "Report of the Bible-Work of the European Turkey Mission, 1883-1884", ABC 16.9, vol. 7.

72. E. M. Stone to N. G. Clark, June 19, 1886, ABC 16.9, vol 9, p. 2.

73. H. C. Haskell, "Quarterly Report of the Samokov Station of the Eu. T. Mission for Sept. 30th, 1896", ABC 16.9, vol. 10; V. Iv. T͡sakova, "Li͡atnoto uchilishte za zheni, dŭrzhano v Samokov ot 9-21 i͡uli", *Zornit͡sa* (Plovdiv), August 12, 1910, pp. 3-4.

74. Strong, pp. 385-386.

75. W. W. Sleeper to J. F. Clarke, March 3, 1883, Clarke Papers.

76. For a description of the revival movement in the European Turkey Mission see, Hall, pp. 66-69; 115-116, 171-173.

77. See Annual Tabular Views for 1882 and 1883 in ABC 16.9, vol. 7.

78. See, for example, Annual Tabular Views for 1887 and 1898 in ABC 16.9, vol. 11, and Annual Tabular View for 1901 and 1902 in ABC 16.9, vol.15.

79. R. Thomson to Dr. Clark, November 28, 1882, ABC 16.9, vol. 9, part 2.

80. Ibid.

81. *Missionary Herald*, May 1916, pp. 228-229.

82. L. Bond to Dr. Clark, January 16, 1871, ABC 16.9, vol. 9, part 2.

83. W. W. Sleeper to Dr. Clark, August 30, 1884, ABC 16.9, vol. 9, part 2.

84. W. W. Sleeper, "Report of Samokov Station, for the year 1884-5", ABC 16.9, vol. 7.

85. E. B. Haskell, "Report of Salonica Station Aug. 1st, 1895-March 25, 1896", Clarke Papers.

86. E. B. Haskell to Martha /Haskell/, December 2, 1901, Haskell Papers.

87. Ibid.

88. F. L. Kingsbury, "Samokov Station Report for the year ending May, 18, 1888", ABC 16.9 vol. 7.

89. E. M. Stone to N. G. Clark, August 31, 1889, ABC 16.9, vol. 9, part 2.

90. L. Bond, "Annual Report of Philippopolis Station for 1878", Clarke Papers.

91. Cited in Hall, p. 70.

92. Elias Riggs, "Report of the Constantinople Station of the European Turkey Mission for year ending April 1, 1898", ABC 16.9, vol. 10.

93. "Table of Statistics for the year ending December 31, 1909", ABC 16.9, vol. 15.

94. J. F. C. 64/3, p. 140, Clarke Papers.

95. W. E. Locke to N. G. Clark, March 13, 1884, ABC 16.9, vol. 9, part 1.

96. J. F. Clarke to N. G. Clark, July 30, 1888, ABC 16.9, vol. 8.

97. "Monastir Touring Experiences", *Missionary News from Bulgaria* 36:5.

98. "Christian Influence", *Missionary News from Bulgaria* 39:3.

99. G. D. Marsh to N. G. Clark, June 20, 1892, ABC 16.9, vol. 14.

100. G. D. Marsh to N. G. Clark, December 21, 1889, ABC 16.9, vol. 9, part 1.

101. H. C. Haskell to N. G. Clark, November 28, 1893, ABC 16.9, vol. 12.

102. E. B. Haskell to Martha, January 8, 1900, Haskell Papers.

103. H. C. Haskell, "Report of the Philippopolis Station for 1906-07," ABC 16.9, vol. 16.

104. Robert Thomson, "The Jubilee of Evangelical Work in European Turkey", *Missionary Herald*, November 1908, p. 502.

105. Edward B. Haskell, *American Influence in Bulgaria*, (Reprinted by permission from the January number of *The*

Missionary Review of the World, New York, n.p., 1919), pp. 6-7.

106. N. G. Clark to F. L. Kingsbury, October 28, 1885, Clarke Papers.

107. J. W. Baird to James L. Barton, August 6, 1895, ABC 16.9, vol. 11.

108. W. E. Locke to N. G. Clark, January 29, 1891, ABC 16.9, vol. 13.

109. W. E. Locke "Records of the 2nd Annual Meeting of the European Turkey Mission," Clarke Papers.

110. J. F. C. 64/3, pp. 140, 159, Clarke Papers.

111. J. W. Baird to N. G. Clark, November 16, 1883, ABC 16.9, vol. 7.

112. G. D. Marsh to N. G. Clark, May 5, 1879, ABC 16.9, vol. 6.

113. J. W. Baird to N. G. Clark, February 28, 1883, ABC 16.9, vol. 7.

114. F. L. Kingsbury to Dr. Judson Smith, October 22, 1895, ABC 16.9, vol. 13.

115. L. F. Ostrander to J. L. Barton, November 30, 1907, ABC 16.9, vol. 20.

116. See, for example, the Estimates for European Turkey Mission in ABC 16.9, vol. 11, and the figures given in the following letters: Judson Smith to Rev. Lewis Bond, November 29, 1901; James L. Barton to Leroy F. Ostrander, November 30, 1904, Haskell Papers; Enoch F. Bell to W. C. Cooper, November 18, 1911, Clarke Papers.

117. H. C. Haskell to Bro. Clarke, January 11, 1896, Clarke Papers.

118. G. D. Marsh to N. G. Clark, September 26, 1891, ABC 16.9, vol. 14.

119. Copy of a letter received April 11 /1902/ by Samokov Station, ABC 16.9, vol. 15.

120. Bulg/arsko/ Propovednichesko Bratstvo do Amerikanskata Misii͡a v Bulgarii͡a i Evropeiska Turtsii͡a, August 30, 1904, Haskell Papers. (It is not clear whether the date is according to the new style.)

121. J. W. Baird, "Report of Monastir Station, Aug. 10, 1895-March 20, 1896," Clarke Papers.

122. *Zorni͡tsa* (Plovdiv), January 17, 1908, p. 4; Mojzes, p. 176.

123. L. Bond, "Report of the Eski Zagra Station for the year ending July 8, 1875," ABC 16.9, vol. 5; J. W. Baird to Brethren of the European Turkey Mission, April 14, 1886 (Annual Report of Monastir Station), Clarke Papers.

124. J. F. C. 64/4, p. 245, Clarke Papers.

125. T. Holway, "Report of Samokove Station," /1906-1907/, ABC 16.9, vol. 16.

126. James T. Barton to Leroy F. Ostrander, January 16, 1905, Haskell Papers.

127. E. B. Haskell to Martha, March 26, 1896, Haskell Papers.

128. R. Thomson to Dr. Clark, May 28, 1884, ABC 16.9, vol. 9, part 2.

129. T. L. Byington to Dr. Clark, June 26, 1875, ABC 16.9, vol. 5.

130. J. F. C. 64/2, pp. 118, 122, Clarke Papers.

131. J. F. C. 64/3, p. 142, Clarke Papers.

132. J. F. C. 64/3, p. 178, Clarke Papers.

133. J. F. C. 64/5, p. 287, Clarke Papers.

134. J. F. Clarke to N. G. Clark, May 12, 1890; J. F. Clarke to N. G. Clark, July 15, 1892, ABC 16.9, vol. 12.

135. "Minutes of the Thirty Fifth Annual Meeting of the European Turkey Mission," ABC 16.9, vol. 15.

136. "Report of Salonica Station. Apr. 29, 1910 to Apr. 19, 1911," Clarke Papers.

137. Edwin M. Bliss to the Members of the Eur. Turkey Mission, April 20, 1886, Clarke Papers.

138. Father to Son /H. C. Haskell to E. B. Haskell/, May 5, 1890, Haskell Papers.

139. H. C. Haskell to E. B. Haskell, March 7, 1890, Haskell Papers.

140. J. W. Baird to N. G. Clark, June 21, 1892, ABC 16.9, vol. 11.

141. See, for example, Stoi͡an Krŭstev Vatralski, *Amerika i Bulgarii͡a*, (Sofia, 1933), pp. 22, 361; D. Mishew, *America and Bulgaria and Their Moral Bonds*, (Bern: Paul Haupt, Akademische Buchhandlung, 1918), p. 9; Tsvetko S. Bagranoff, *The American Missions' Share in the Regeneration and Defense of Bulgaria*, (American Bulgarian Good Neighbor League, 1947), p. 3.

142. Liuben Karavelov, *Sŭbrani suchineniia*, vol. 7, (Sofia, 1967), p. 119.

143. A. Shopov, *Bulgariia v tsŭrkovno otnoshenie,* (Plovdiv, 1889), p. 13.

144. *Makedoniia* (Constantinople), December, 1871.

145. M. Stoianov, "Petko R. Slaveikov i protestanskata propaganda u nas," *Rodina* 3 (March, 1941): 97; Veselin Traikov, "Protestantskite misioneri i borbata na bŭlgarskiia narod za tsŭrkovna svoboda," *Bulgariia v sveta ot drevnostta do nashi dni*, vol. 1, (Sofia, 1979), p. 467.

CHAPTER II
MISSIONARY EDUCATION

1. *Bulgarian Demand for Education*

*...the Bulgarian, confessing his ignorance, asks to be instructed and enlightened**

In their early contacts with the Bulgarians, the first American missionaries to settle south of the Balkan Mountains immediately noticed the great importance that natives placed on education. The accelerating process of National Revival among the Bulgarians was manifested, among other things, in a desire for knowledge and for personal improvement. From the very beginning of missionary involvement in the region, the representatives of the American Board regularly encountered and took notice of this frequently expressed desire.

In 1860, following a tour in the area surrounding Eski Zagra, T. L. Byington reported that "the more intelligent Bulgarians are idolizing education," yet they did not show any interest in "spiritual things."(1) This early observation expressed the essence of numerous subsequent missionary reports which emphasized the Bulgarian desire for education but education of a secular type. The same missionary concluded two years after his earlier remark that "the Bulgarians evidently intend to get as much secular and as little religious instruction from us as possible."(2) This time Byington's statement came as a result of the experience of the first American missionary school for girls in Eski Zagra. Apparently, the Bulgarian students there ignored the attempt of the missionaries to begin religious services for them.(3) Nor did the parents of these girls appreciate the Americans' highest aim—to influence the Bulgarians in terms of religion, of spirituality. In 1865, for example, these natives made a gesture of kindness toward the teacher in the missionary school by

* J. N. Ball to R. Anderson, August 30, 1865, ABC 16.9, v. 4.

presenting her with "a handsome silk dress. . .as an expression of their gratitude." The parents addressed a letter to the American Board expressing "their grateful acknowledgement for its efforts in behalf of female education in Bulgaria." The missionary who received the letter, however, quickly noted that "no gratitude has been expressed. . .for our efforts in behalf of the spiritual good of their children."(4)

This "one-sidedness," at least from the missionary point of view, in the Bulgarian understanding and demand for education continued to be noted in American writings during the following years. For example, at the school for boys which was opened in 1860 at Philippopolis, Rev. J. F. Clarke noted that most of the students "have entered the school mainly for the sake of an education and without any desire for the gospel."(5) This report, dated 1869, confirmed previously expressed concerns about the nature of the Bulgarian desire for education. At the headquarters of the American Board in Boston, this concern eventually grew into a rather unpleasant expectation that such a desire for education would only hinder the accomplishment of the main missionary goal in Bulgaria. In the words of Secretary N. G. Clark: "The people are bewildered now with the idea of education as the all important thing, instead of the gospel. It is a mistake that will stand in our way."(6)

Indeed, wherever and whenever the missionaries brought their activity to different Bulgarian settlements, they observed the same intense interest in education for its own sake and not for religious improvement. In 1899, H. E. Cole, an American teacher at the school for girls at Monastir voiced an opinion which repeated previous missionary statements regarding the Bulgarian desire for education: "The people are alive as regards education, but have never yet shown any real interest in the religious part of our work."(7)

The Bulgarians, on their part, did not find anything wrong with their willingness to get an education wherever available. They often approached the Americans with very concrete and definite ideas about the best way the missionaries might act. For instance, leading figures among the Bulgarians in Istanbul approached Rev. J. F. Clarke in 1861, and in their list of proposals, requested that the Protestants open a girls' school.(8) This query was also repeated in Philippopolis, where representatives of the Bulgarian population wanted to get American help "in the establishment of a Seminary for young men and a school for girls."(9) During the 1870's, with the opening of more and more places for missionary activity aimed at the Bulgarians, this behavior continued. In the Monastir region, the first Americans were usually met with questions about possible educational opportunities. One of the participants left the following account of the typical Bulgarian approach: "The question oftenest asked is 'When are you intending to open a school.' They take it for granted that we have come here to hold schools and teach sciences and languages."(10)

This understanding of what a missionary was supposed to do did not coincide with that of the Americans'. Clearly, the natives perceived the missionaries more as educators* than proselytizers. This aspect of the Bulgarian attitude was not lost on the missionaries themselves and caused the latter a good deal of frustration. As the missionary residing in Monastir, J. W. Baird expressed his feelings in a letter, dated February 1874: "It is strange that they /the natives/ can't comprehend it when we tell them 'No. We didn't come here to teach Eng/lish/ but to preach the Gospel'."(11) Apparently, the Bulgarian population saw itself generally in need of education but not in need of Protestant Christianity. This possibly explains the initial welcome that the Bulgarians extended to the missionaries—a welcome to people who might offer them good "Western" education and not to people offering a new type of Christianity. This mistaken image of the American Board missionaries was most likely due, in addition to the genuine need for a better education among the Bulgarians, to an initial Bulgarian ignorance of missionary goals. Also, previous Western missionaries, such as the Catholics, first stressed the educational aspect of their work.(12)

Whether because of precedent or misunderstanding, the Bulgarian population clearly expressed that it expected

* The same perception of the American missionaries persists in the works of present-day Bulgarian historians. In a recent doctoral dissertation, for example, the following statement was made: "The missionaries in Bulgaria were not only preachers, they fulfilled the functions of specially trained teachers who aided the advancing Bulgarian education." See, Andrei Pantev, "Bŭlgarskii͡at vŭpros v Anglii͡a i SASHT 1876-1903," (Ph.D. dissertation, SU "Kliment Okhridski," 1984), pp. 44-45.

education from the missionaries. And whenever education was forthcoming, the Bulgarians did not hesitate to show their appreciation. The missionaries themselves acknowledged that the natives "were grateful for the aid given them in education."(13) The fact that leading Bulgarian families would send their children to missionary schools was also an indication that there was general acceptance of the Americans in their capacity as educators. The example of the girls' school in Eski Zagra might be considered. According to accounts by a contemporary who was reading missionary publications "with joy," the most prominent families in the city sent their daughters to the American Missionary school because there was no school any better.(14)

The missionaries noted and understood the Bulgarians' demand for education during the second half of the last century. Early in their stay among the Bulgarians, the representatives of the American Board realized the possibility of gaining the respect and gratitude of the native population by offering it the much sought after learning. At the same time, they knew that the missionary style of education would not be widely acceptable. Still, the opportunity, the demand was there. It remained to be decided whether the missionaries were willing to involve themselves in the job of educating the emerging Bulgarian nation.

2. *Education and Evangelization*

At the time of the first contacts between missionaries and Bulgarians, the native clamor for education did not mean that there were no Bulgarian schools. The process of creating secular schools that could offer a more modern education had already begun in the Bulgarian lands during the first half of the nineteenth century. It is known, for example, that from 1835 to 1878, 1,658 secular schools were opened in Bulgaria,(15) and more than 200 of them had existed prior to 1850, the latter being schools which applied the Lancasterian educational system. (16) Those schools produced a literate public, but its percentage, given the size of the entire Bulgarian population, was probably not high. Even with the lack of precise information, it is evident that there was a degree of literacy among the Bulgarians* and that they had taken into their own hands the task of educating themselves. In other words, the missionaries were not faced with a completely illiterate population which had to be taught, at the very least, to read in order to make it a potential subject of evangelization. The nature of Protestantism presupposes literacy among its followers. In Bulgaria, schools were already in existence when the missionaries arrived. That was why the question of whether to engage in educating a very willing population did not have a simple answer. The missionaries had to decide what the role of education would be in the work of converting the Bulgarians to Protestantism. Given the willingness of the natives to receive instruction, the missionaries resolved this question in a positive manner soon after their arrival.

In August 1862, the American Board gave its permission to the missionaries working among the Bulgarians to open two schools, one for girls and one for boys. This was done after repeated pleas on behalf of the missionaries to that effect. T. L. Byington acted as a spokesman to his colleagues, and in his letters to Boston, he expressed the feeling among the missionaries that schools would be the best avenue toward achieving the missionary objective. According to Byington, residing among the natives convinced all missionaries

> that our work among the Bulgarians will be difficult to prosecute. . .We are all of one mind in regarding a school for girls as one of the most hopeful means, that, in the present condition of our work, could be made use of.(17)

In this case, the future school for girls in Eski Zagra was in question. In other communications to Boston, Byington took the task of making known the consensus among his coworkers in relation to the general problem of the role of education in this particular missionary enterprise. A month before the

* The American missionaries considered that there were "probably half a million if not two thirds who can read" among the Bulgarians; see, C. F. Morse, "Report of Adrianople Station," ABC 16.9, v. 4. Unfortunately, there is no reliable statistical information about the degree of literacy among the Bulgarian population during the middle of the nineteenth century.

decision of the American Board, he summed up their feelings as follows:

> I think all of the brethren felt that schools were an agency which could not be dispensed with in the prosecution of our work among the Bulgarians. And I ...fear that if we are not permitted to open them, our mission to this people will prove a failure.(18)

In the early 1860s, the missionaries considered educational endeavors to be the key to their success among the Bulgarians. The Americans thought that by offering schools they would gain access to the natives' souls which could not be secured in any other manner. Education was thus seen as a means to approach the main task of the mission and not as a way to prepare the people for Protestantism by giving them the basic skills of reading and writing. The expectation was that only by supplying the one thing that the Bulgarians wanted most — education — could the missionaries penetrate the barrier between the natives and themselves. A special committee which was formed to study the question of opening Bulgarian schools at the Western Turkey Mission, reported in June 1862, regarding a school for boys at Philippopolis, that it "will be the most economical mode of getting access to the people." Calculating that at this early stage of missionary involvement among the Bulgarians the cost of gaining one hearer was roughly one thousand dollars, while the cost to the mission for one student would be only thirty-five dollars, the committee was eager to impress upon the American Board that schools were the "door of entrance to the people."(19)

Following the opening of the school for girls early in 1863, Byington continued his enthusiastic support of this institution and again strongly suggested to Boston that no hope of converting the Bulgarians could be entertained without the existence of missionary schools. Writing on behalf of the Eski Zagra Station, he concluded: "The experience of the past year /1863/ has confirmed us in the opinion that the most effective agency we can employ at this station for the evangelization of the Bulgarians is our female school."(20) A strong tendency was thus exhibited to replace traditional methods of evangelizing (such as preaching) by educational efforts. Certainly this flexibility was due, to a large extent, to the careful observation of the peculiarities of the natives. In the process of acquiring more and more direct knowledge about them, the missionaries were willing to accommodate certain Bulgarian desires.

With the accumulation of further experience in the educational sphere, however, the missionaries began to voice new opinions regarding the relationship between educational work and evangelization. Rev. J. F. Clarke made it clear in 1865 that he had not regarded the schools "as indispensable in *gaining* /Clarke's emphasis/ a foothold" among the Bulgarians. Rather, he had considered them "a desirable experiment." At the time he expressed his views, he urged direct evangelizing by preaching and prayer and not by educating the natives. (21) He did not completely reject the schools but saw them as the agency which would provide native Protestant leaders. More specifically, in regard to the school for boys which was started in Philippopolis he explained that the missionaries at Philippopolis had never intended to make it the main thrust of their work. The school was intended to prepare those who wanted a theological education and to influence by example the remainder of the natives. (22)

During the next decades, more and more missionaries began to doubt the necessity of the now even more firmly established system of missionary schools. Some, like J. W. Baird, completely denied any use for the schools. In 1873, he wrote: "Education for which there is some clamor. . .can do nothing of itself but furnish better material for Satan to use." (23) A certain fear of spoiling the virtues of the simple natives by educating them might be detected in these lines. At the same time, this particular missionary did not believe that American education might play an evangelizing role in Bulgaria.

Others were not so extreme in their judgement but were concerned that the missionaries were allowing themselves to be overly influenced by the Bulgarians' pronounced interest in education. G. D. Marsh, who spent most of his missionary life in Philippopolis, shared the following view of the European Turkey Mission with one of the secretaries of the American Board:

> In our Mission work we seem to put such honor on our schools. . .that it is having a most injurious effect. The

> *nation* respects schools, and teaching... *We* respect such work... The *nation* neglects, or despises the preaching of the Gospel, and by our not giving more time and strength to evangelistic work our Bulgarian friends seem to think that *we* do not honor such work in any such degree as I *know* we all do. (24) /all emphasis by Marsh/

In Marsh's view, education in the field received a disproportionate emphasis which aided the Bulgarians' obvious esteem of learning for its own sake. Clearly, evangelization was suffering due to the great attention given to educating the Bulgarians. More importantly, the Bulgarians were forming a false impression about the real intentions of the missionaries. Marsh's discontent with missionary policies and actions was echoed by a colleague, W. E. Locke. According to Locke, the great emphasis on education among the Americans was influencing their native followers: in the region of Philippopolis, almost every Protestant community was disposed "to enlarge its expenditure for educational purposes at the cost of what they give for preaching." (25) In fact, judging from the figures reflecting payments by the Bulgarians at the time the statement was made and during subsequent years, the natives always gave much more for preaching than for school purposes. The figures for the entire mission in 1891, when Locke made the above statement, showed that the amount given for preaching was 2.65 times larger than the one given for schools. (26) Clearly, Locke's observation did not correspond to reality. Allowing for regional differences, however, and for expectations by the missionaries that payments made for preaching should be much larger than what were actually given, it is possible to understand Locke's concern.

One point is clear, nevertheless—some missionaries no longer considered education to be the most effective way of accomplishing the great task of converting the Bulgarian nation. With the maturing of the missionary enterprise, including its educational aspects, they began to look upon education as a distraction from their main goal. This opinion was expressed by at least three men. The initial consensus no longer existed in missionary thinking regarding their educational efforts.

In order to better understand this occurrence, it is useful to consider what educational endeavors the missionaries undertook during the last four decades of the nineteenth and the first decade of the twentieth century.

3. *Missionary Education for the Bulgarians*

The first school the missionaries opened for Bulgarian youth was a "school for young men" in Philippopolis. It was started in September-October 1860* with just two Bulgarian youths, the number of students increasing during the school year to eleven boarders and two so-called "dayschoolers." The institution was planned to be a four-year boarding school for boys. (27) Initially, the only stated requirements were for the applicants not to be "immoral in their lives," to know how to read and to "furnish their own clothing." As the Americans themselves acknowledged, "the great inducement for scholars" to come to the school was the fact that education and board were free.(28) On July 8, 1869, the school was closed following a decision at the above mentioned Convention of Bulgarian Missionaries held in March 1869. At this meeting, it was recommended that a new school for boys be organized "for instruction of pious youth who give promise of being useful helpers in some department" of missionary work.(29) A class of students fitting the new requirements was begun in September 1870, in Eski Zagra and transferred the next year to Samokov.(30) This city became the permanent home of the school which went through several changes but which finally came to be known as the American Collegiate and Theological Institute (hereafter, the Institute) in 1880-1881.(31) The history of this school has already been described.(32) Therefore, the present chapter will emphasize only a few central developments in the history of the school which will contribute to a better understanding of the role of education in the work of the European Turkey Mission.

Once transferred to Samokov, the Institute began to accept two types of natives as students: one was made up of so called "charity students" who were required to work "two years (under fitting pay) under the direction of the Missionaries" for

* The school was opened prior to receiving formal permission by the American Board.

each year that they spent in the school; the other group was composed of students who were willing to pay for the education offered by the missionaries.(33) Offering financial aid to willing students was eventually abandoned in favor of self-help. Thus, in 1886 an Industrial Department was initiated at the Institute which offered the opportunity of earning money and gaining vocational training at the same time. The Industrial Department was divided into two sections: printing and woodwork.(34) The school's curriculum underwent numerous changes, too, which finally led to its recognition by the Bulgarian authorities as equivalent to the Bulgarian gymnasium. This occurred in 1915, (35) but despite the relative lateness of the events, the recognition was an important acknowledgement of significant changes in the Institute's course of study.

The course of study in the Institute was originally divided into two sections—the first was the so-called "scientific" course, and following its completion, those who wished might enter the second, a "theological" course. This division was preserved throughout the entire period under consideration, with the significant changes being made in the "scientific" course. By 1908-1909, the latter was a seven-year course following the model of the Bulgarian gymnasium. It was supplemented by the traditional one-year theological course.(36)

The Institute produced 83 graduates in the scientific course during the first fifty years of missionary involvement among the Bulgarians. According to calculations done by H. C. Haskell, in 1908 thirty-five of these graduates had taken the theological course and eighteen of them had become preachers or pastors.(37)

Two boarding schools for girls were also opened and maintained by the missionaries. The above mentioned school for girls in Eski Zagra was begun in January 1863, with a three-year course of study. During its first year, the school attracted some twenty students.(38) Simultaneous with the transfer of the school for boys to Samokov, the Eski Zagra institution was moved to the same location, opening at Samokov on September 12, 1871.(39) The curriculum of the school for the first ten years of its existence was that of an elementary school with Bible instruction, the three-year course being increased by one year.(40)

Gradually, changes in the program of study were made to parallel more or less the changes at the Institute. The goal of both institutions was identical—to gain recognition by the Bulgarian authorities as equivalent to the state's respective female and male national gymnasiums. The girls' boarding school began to offer a course of study closely corresponding to the one at the female Bulgarian gymnasium in 1902/1903. During that school year, the principal of the American school reported the existence of a three-year kindergarten and a four-year primary department, which were followed by a six-year course of study corresponding to the one at the Bulgarian gymnasiums.(41) Eventually, the government recognized these programs in July 1914, a year before they extended such recognition to the Institute.(42)

The name of the school for girls underwent changes, too. In 1880-1881 it was reformulated from the initial Female Boarding School to Girl's Boarding School.(43)

The acceptance policies of the school for girls were quite similar to the ones at the Institute. All boarders had to pay a minimum fee, and those who received substantial financial aid pledged to work a year in missionary employ for each year of aid.(44) At this institution, however, no developments similar to the creation of the Industrial Department at the Institute occurred.

After the early 1870's, Samokov could claim to be the educational center by supporting two institutions of higher learning. The Girl's Boarding School produced its share of graduates, and in 1908, Samokov was able to report 124 girl graduates distributed among 23 graduating classes. These graduates supplied the Mission with 42 Biblewomen and 69 teachers. (45)

The Samokov educational endeavors did not exhaust all missionary effort on behalf of Bulgarian education. Other components of the missionary educational activity included two more institutions of higher learning—one, the second boarding school for girls, at Monastir, and the other at Salonica—a kindergarten at Sofia, and a number of so-called common schools and Sunday schools*.

* Sunday schools are regarded here in their capacity of educational institutions. It is acknowledged that they might be considered also as a means of direct evangelization; however, due to their structured approach to learning, they are viewed from the educational point of view.

Monastir became a location for the second American boarding school for girls in 1881.(46) This school followed in the steps of its Samokov predecessor and was aimed at natives, not necessarily Bulgarians, of the Bulgarian regions that remained under Turkish authority after 1878. The majority of the girls who entered the school, as well as the native teachers, were Bulgarian. The official language of the school was changed from Bulgarian to English in 1898/1899 in order to widen the appeal of the school, but most of the students and all of the native teachers were of Bulgarian nationality.(47) In 1908, H. C. Haskell calculated that the school had produced 35 graduates from the time of its opening until 1908, but he did not specify their nationalities. All but three worked for a time as evangelical teachers.(48)

Salonica was the other station of the European Turkey Mission that initiated a school for the natives residing in the Ottoman Empire. This school was organized in 1904 on a 52 acre farm which the missionaries had previously purchased. Ten orphan boys were the first scholars. The farm school was incorporated under the laws of the state of New York in October 1904 and was known as The Thessalonica Agricultural and Industrial Institute.(49) The students divided their time equally between work and study, the course of study modeled again after the curriculum of the Bulgarian gymnasium. The work that the students were expected to do fell under several departments—agriculture, carpentry and masonry, shoemaking, and tailoring.(50) This innovative school did not draw financial aid from the American Board because it received outside help and also because it could more than cover its own expenses by the end of the period considered.(51) Nevertheless, the very existence of the school was made possible only because of the planning and leadership of the missionaries at Salonica. No information about graduates is available, possibly due to the relative newness of the institution which existed only eight years before the start of the Balkan Wars.

Missionary initiative was responsible for still another undertaking and innovation in the education of native youth. In 1898, Elizabeth C. Clarke, daughter of Rev. J. F. Clarke, started as her own project a kindergarten at Samokov.(52) This school was moved to Sofia in October 1900 and had an enrollment of 76 children during 1908/1909.(53) Along with preschool education, the institution offered training classes for kindergarten teachers for the first time in Bulgaria. By 1912/1913, Elizabeth Clarke had two trained assistants, and three members in the training class.(54)

The common schools in the different locations varied greatly. Often they were simply Protestant elementary schools, or sometimes evening classes were organized depending on the needs of the community. These schools were, as a rule, staffed only by native teachers. Together with the Sunday schools, they represented the less visible part of missionary educational efforts. No reports, except numerical, were kept of this work, hence only a statistical view of the mass education supplied by the European Turkey Mission may be ventured. All available data is arranged in Table 2 which represents the period 1870-1909. Occasional missing years indicate that no complete data for them were found. The term "educational facilities" comprises all schools run by missionaries or native helpers, except the Sunday schools which are presented separately. The blank spaces for the number of Sunday schools are again due to the unavailability of information.

The statistical data confirm the previously expressed missionary opinion of the significant role education had to play in the Bulgarian work. If we compared the number of schools and number of churches /see, Table 1/ for any year when information is available, it becomes clear that the European Turkey Mission always had more schools than churches for the Bulgarians. During the twenty-seven years for which such a comparison can be done (1875, 1881-1884, 1886, 1887, 1889-1896, 1898-1909), the average yearly ratio between schools and churches was approximately 1.8:1. During the last decade of that period, the ratio was not significantly lower, 1.6:1.

The figures given for the number of native teachers employed by the Mission and the ordained native helpers present an even clearer picture of the predominance of the educational element in missionary work. A comparison of those figures can be done for twenty-six years (1875, 1881-1884, 1887, 1889-1896, 1898-1909). For each year, on the average, there were 3.3 native teachers for every ordained

TABLE 2*

STATISTICAL RESULTS: EDUCATION (1870-1909)

YEAR	NATIVE TEACHERS	EDUCATIONAL FACILITIES	STUDENTS	SUNDAY SCHOOLS	SUNDAY SCHOOL MEMBERSHIP
1870	4	1	15	5	104
1875	8	6	117	13	367
1876	10	6	103	9	385
1880[a]	9	15	454	18	849
1881[a]	13	12	435	18	858
1882[a]	9	14	452	19	998
1883[a]	10	11	389	15	838
1886	16	15	633	23	889
1887	20	11	663		1251
1889	19	17	597	14	1497
1890	31	19	687		1411
1891	31	19	652		1584
1892	29	21	768		1597
1893	23	22	718		1741
1894	35	21	684		1886
1895	35	20	656		2014
1896	34	20	573		1864
1898	30	22	688	43	2138
1899	38	23	665		2291
1900	39	24	657	53	2379
1901	43	22	787	55	2983
1902	50	26	829	56	2719
1903	57	31	959	52	2630
1904	54	25	922	52	2596
1905	50	29	861	51	2482
1906	51	29	820	53	2535
1907	55	29	847	54	2584
1908	60	30	847	56	2583
1909	55	27	866	57	2578

*All the information compiled in Table 2 may be found in Tabular Views for the respective years in ABC 16.9, vols. 4, 7, 11, 15. The data for 1875/1876 was taken from a Tabular View in the Clarke Papers.

[a]For year ending March 31.

native worker. The same comparison for the last decade of the period was only slightly lower, 3.2:1.

The above calculations help substantiate previously mentioned concerns by certain missionaries that the work among the Bulgarians overemphasized the educational element at the expense of the evangelical one. The comparison made for the years 1900-1909 further demonstrate that this tendency was not being overcome with the passage of time. It is apparent that the initial hope of the missionaries that education would "open doors" to the otherwise unapproachable Bulgarians was not fulfilled. The natives certainly showed interest in education, but this did not lead to a marked increase of interest in Protestantism. In contrast with the grievances concerning the lack of preachers among the natives, the Americans did not have any trouble finding enough teachers to hire. No complaints about scarcity of teachers for the missionary schools were found in the voluminous documents left behind by the Americans. It seems that the education offered by the European Turkey Mission could produce teachers but not as many preachers and pastors. Furthermore, the distribution of graduates from the three schools in Samokov and Monastir definitely supports this observation (see pages 65-67).

A comparison between the number of students and the number of church members (see Table 1), however, modifies the view that the missionaries had failed in their use of education as an agency of evangelization. While no one should dispute the fact that American Protestantism had an insignificant impact on Bulgarian society from a numerical point of view, the limited influence that it did have may have been due to the schools. Only in the late 1880's was the number of students in missionary schools lower than the number of church members. A possible explanation for this might indeed be the "door-opening" effect of education among the Bulgarians. It is logical to assume that the three decades from 1860 to the end of the 1880's were decades when education was the more powerful vehicle of missionary influence than direct evangelizing efforts.

It is not possible to find sufficient information regarding the number of students who attended the missionary schools during the period discussed*, which makes unfeasible the otherwise interesting comparison between the number of church members in 1909, for example, and the number of students that had attended missionary schools up to that point. Still, the comparisons that were previously made warrant by themselves the observation that the European Turkey Mission found it easier to work as an educational agency than as a purely religious one.

A look at the development of the Sunday school institution in the European Turkey field provides a different perspective on the role of education in the Mission. The Sunday schools seem to have been the most popular type of missionary education among the Bulgarians. They clearly outnumber the other schools in quantity and in membership. The same tendency, in fact, is observed in comparison with the number of Protestant churches and their membership (see Table 1). This correlation seems to indicate that strictly religious missionary instruction was the most welcomed by the natives. On the other hand, we should note that no references to that effect were found in missionary writing. Possibly, these figures may be explained by the fact that Sunday schools do not require much financial outlay or highly trained teachers. As a result, the missionaries were able to offer those classes much more regularly. In addition, Sunday school attendance was significantly easier for the natives; proclaiming themselves Protestant was a major decision, attending Sunday school was not. In any case, the relative popularity of the Sunday schools would substantiate the opinion that education, even a religious one, was more acceptable to the Bulgarians than the American Board's brand of Christianity.

One final observation should be made regarding the data in Table 2: even though the growth of missionary educational endeavors was quite impressive,** the last decade represented in the table shows signs of possible saturation and even stagnation. This is especially true for the number of students

* Information was found only for the Institute at Samokov. According to missionary calculations: "Up to June 1910, nearly 800 different students have been in the school." See L. F. Ostrander, ed., *Fifty Years in Bulgaria*, (Samokov, 1911), p. 48.

** The number of students, for example, increased more than 57 times from 1870 to 1909, and the Sunday school membership grew almost 25 times.

and the Sunday school membership, which overall demonstrated a most impressive rate of growth.

The statistical analysis of the available data readily illustrates the emphasis on education in the work of the European Turkey Mission. As previously shown, at least a portion of the missionaries found this development disturbing. In spite of such concerns, however, the missionary staff attempted to look at the results of their educational activities in order to determine what their schools had accomplished among the Bulgarians. Such a critic of missionary educational "excesses" as G. D. Marsh, for example, made observations which indicate that American education was widely considered an institution of impact among the Bulgarians. In 1898, he wrote: "Our reputation and influence in the Balkan Peninsula is based upon our Educational. . .work rather than upon the strictly Evangelistic."(55) More specifically, Marsh regarded the missionary schools to have exercised "an indirect beneficial influence by stimulating the Bulgarian people to learn our /the American/ educational methods and to organize its own schools at many places."(56)

Marsh's opinion tends to place the results of American missionary education in a nonreligious sphere by pointing to the alleged influence that the missionary schools had on the general development of Bulgarian education. At the same time, Marsh seems to regard the evolving system of education in the Bulgarian lands as decidedly influenced by the American model.* Such a tendency to overestimate their own influence was not characteristic of all missionaries. Following the First World War, E. B. Haskell felt the need to repudiate all claims which implied that Bulgaria owed its educational system to the Americans. He felt that the role of the missionary schools was much more modest and that these institutions simply contributed to the intellectual advance of the Bulgarians.(57) Other missionary writings emphasized the role of their best schools as training future leaders and

* Actually, the Bulgarian system of education was modeled on European examples. The influence of the missionary schools was more of a supplementary source of education which by its mere existence stimulated native educational efforts. As explained by a scholar of that region: "Mere rivalry did much to hasten the educational development of all the Christian races", including the Bulgarians, in particular, among those. See, H. H. Brailsford, *Macedonia. Its Races and Their Future*, (New York: Arno Press and The New York Times, 1971), p. 74.

influential people in Bulgaria. A publication commemorating the sixtieth anniversary of the Samokov schools stated that about two thousand students were sent from these schools to take "positions of leadership and wide influence in the country."(58) These claims were somewhat contradicted, however, by the fact that the same publication named only ten such people "of influence," five of whom were primarily important to the small Protestant community and not necessarily to the rest of the nation.(59)

All these highly positive evaluations of their own efforts to educate the Bulgarians neglected to consider the evangelical aspect of missionary intentions. Originally, the schools were planned as the most effective way of approaching the Bulgarians. Following years of much work and money spent on education, the Americans viewed their efforts in a different light. The schools were no longer opening doors among the Bulgarians but supposedly producing people of influence for the natives.

Regarding the question of the training of qualified helpers, the results were not particularly encouraging. Marsh, who could hardly be called a promoter of education among the missionaries, reported in 1912 that the schools did not properly serve the needs of the Mission:

> In the passing of the years. . .we have increased the educational institutions of our church. And the more that they have increased, and the more expensive they become, the fewer workers do they supply. . .(60)

A definite discrepancy is evident between the goals of the missionaries in opening their schools and the way in which they decided to evaluate the role of these schools. The evangelical aspect was no longer important, possibly due to disappointing results. Instead, education for the Bulgarians was appreciated for what was perceived to be a general beneficial effect on Bulgarian society. The same point of view characterizes the historiography on that subject. Repeating, in essence, missionary pronouncements, historians generally agree that "educational missions have constituted the most effective means of service and instrument of progress."(61) The Samokov schools, in particular, were viewed by one researcher as "the most important American institution in Bulgaria."(62)

Similar to the manner in which they regarded evangelizing efforts, the missionaries viewed their educational work from the perspective of the entire Bulgarian people. In evaluating this work, the Americans did not adhere to their original intentions for opening schools. Instead, they separated the evangelizing aspect of their educational work from the overall results of the work and thus were able to claim significant influence among the Bulgarians. Their accomplishments, in other words, were divorced from the initial goals of their educational activities.

4. *Missionary Education and the Bulgarians*

The Bulgarian attitude toward the American educational facilities varied from 1858 to 1912-1913. The enthusiasm for missionary education modified and eventually shrank with the development of a superior, state-supported system of education in the new Bulgarian state. The highly dynamic Revival period in Bulgarian history, which was the background for missionary activities, put the Americans in a competitive position regarding the national educational effort. Originally, the quality of missionary education was not questioned and was regarded as superior. The school for boys at Philippopolis, for example, was the first school in Bulgaria where chemical and physical experiments were performed.(63) Following its transfer to Samokov, the same institution had a well-equipped chemical laboratory.(64) The male students in Samokov were involved in different, more or less innovative, activities. They collected old manuscripts in the region of Macedonia, for example; they participated in the school's own fire-fighting company; they collected fossils which were sent to universities in Europe, the United States, and the Bulgarian Principality.(65)

In spite of such a modern and progressive approach to education, the missionaries had entered a competition they could not win. The missionary schools were no match for the evolving educational system in Bulgaria in terms of financial support, teachers, buildings, and so on. During the 1880's, the first signs of the relative inadequacy of missionary education appeared. In Macedonia, where the Bulgarian government maintained schools through the Exarchate and was competing with the Greeks, Serbians, and Romanians,* one of the Americans remarked in 1883 that American education was no longer necessary. In the words of this missionary, the Mission was "being relieved of the educational part of the work of elevating this /the Bulgarian/ people."(66)

The native followers saw these developments in a different light. They began to criticize the missionary schools and demanded improvement. In the spring of 1888, at a conference of evangelical workers, the Bulgarian Protestants voiced "some criticism of Protestant schools, especially primary, that while far ahead of the other Bulgarian schools in moral training they were far behind the latter in mental training."(67) The negative feeling on the part of these natives was understandable since their own children attended these schools. Even the Bulgarian public, however, began to express critical opinions of the American schools. In 1889, for example, one of the missionary women described an article from an unspecified Bulgarian newspaper which read to the effect that "our /the missionary/ methods are all out-of-date and that in examination we put the answer into the mouth of the pupil."(68)

Matters became especially difficult for the missionaries following the adoption of a new Bulgarian law in December 1891 which held that students graduating from private schools (which included the missionary schools) had to pass examinations at the national schools in order to acquire the same rights as graduates of the national schools. Commenting on the effects of this law, H. C. Haskell reported that the number of students at the Samokov schools was diminishing; in addition, he acknowledged that the course of study in those schools was "not as thorough and complete in some subjects as that of the gymnasia."(69) The same problem existed at the school for girls at Monastir where the American teacher, M. L. Matthews, conceded that the American schools "can offer

* The following is J. W. Baird's description of educational competition in Macedonia:

> The Bulgarians through the Exarch spend in Macedonia each year about 25,000 liras in support of teachers and schools. . .The Greeks too used to spend about that sum yearly, but now their finances are low. The Roumanians spend several thousand liras and the Servians too would be glad to do a similar thing.

See, J. W. Baird to James L. Barton, March 26, 1895, ABC 16.9, vol. 11.

nothing better from an intellectual standpoint" compared to the Bulgarian and Greek schools in the area.(70)

Opinions among the Bulgarians continued to be critical of the quality of missionary education—even more so than the views of the missionaries. The superintendent of the Bulgarian exhibit at the Chicago World Fair in 1893, V. Shopov, met and conversed with leading men of the American Board regarding the Institute at Samokov. In his opinion, "the national Gymnasia were so good schools now that the boys" in the Institute might be sent there for secular education.(71) It followed naturally that the Institute would not be needed except for religious education which was given in the one-year theological course of study.

During the next decade, the missionaries received a formal letter from a native organization of preachers which voiced the following complaint:

> We feel that the Collegiate and Theological Institute at Samokov. . .had not kept with the constantly improving native schools, and neither answers to the needs of the country, nor strengthens the Evangelical cause in Bulgaria.(72)

The opinion of the Bulgarian teachers at the Institute was even more negative. In 1905, a report by these teachers concluded that the graduates of the Institute "are considered as strangers in Bulgaria" and were generally absent from all public office.(73) The same report contained a rather despondent question, which might even be applied to the entire activity of the European Turkey Mission: "Is it worth while to spend our lives and energies almost for nothing; doing, perhaps, a good deal, but accomplishing nothing?"(74)

Certainly, a great variety of people criticized the missionary schools. Beginning in the 1880s and continuing to the early 1900s, Bulgarians, both Protestant and non-Protestant, missionaries, and teachers were pressing for the improvement of the American schools or the closing of the same as being inferior to the national schools. As mentioned earlier, the Samokov schools indeed changed their curriculum and were eventually recognized as equivalent to the national gymnasiums. This was done because of native competition in education and the awareness among American and Bulgarian Protestants that the missionary schools should be improved.

A curious reversal of roles may be observed in the history of the American schools in Bulgaria. At the beginning, these schools were thought to stimulate the native schools. However, with the establishment of the national system of education in Bulgaria, the native schools were the ones that stimulated the advancement of the missionary schools.

Due to this peculiarity in the development of the schools of the European Turkey Mission, the great differences found in the contemporary and subsequent Bulgarian evaluation of these institutions is not surprising. The opinions among the natives varied widely. Some, probably best exemplified by a pro-American Bulgarian publicist, Dimitŭr Mishev, regarded missionary influence as decisive for the very existence of Bulgarian education. According to him, "in her initiative in opening and sustaining schools, Bulgaria is wholly the child of America."*(75) At the opposite end of the Bulgarian understanding of missionary education stood the earlier mentioned T. Ikonomov who regarded the American schools in Bulgaria as lacking quality.(76)

These two extremes in the native view regarding the schools of the European Turkey Mission, however, do not correctly represent the general tone of most Bulgarian writings on that question. The scholarly approach to that subject from the end of the nineteenth century to the present is unanimous

* Opinions like Mishev's and a previously mentioned one originating from G. D. Marsh (see page 72) resulted in a tendency among scholars to regard the Bulgarian Revival as resulting from missionary activity. P. Mojzes, for example, wrote that the missionaries and their native helpers were "one of the major sources of the renaissance of the Bulgarian vernacular literature and language" (see, Mojzes, p. 625). While referring to a sphere of missionary activity that will be discussed in the next chapter, this statement is still characteristic of a portion of the Western historiography on that subject. The Bulgarian scholars refute statements like this, and, in fact, some of the missionaries were the first to point out that the Bulgarian Revival made possible missionary activity, and not the other way around. J. H. House, for instance, in a report from Eski Zagra, wrote that "the awakening among the people" made conditions for missionary work "exceedingly favorable" (see, J. Henry House, "Report of Eski Zagra Station for the year ending June 18th 1874," Clarke Papers). Perhaps, the best expression of this thought came from a close friend of the missionaries, the President of the well-known Robert College, George Washburn. In 1883 he wrote:

> It was no American influence which roused the Bulgarians from the sleep of five centuries to a consciousness of their ignorance... On the contrary, it was the report of this awakening which reached America through Dr. Hamlin, which led to the establishment of the missions. (See, George Washburn, "Religious Liberty in Bulgaria," *The Independent* 35:2).

in acknowledging the positive influence of American education on the cultural emancipation of the Bulgarian nation. Thus, Prof. Ivan Shishmanov wrote in 1898 that the American Protestants had really contributed to the development of the field of education in Bulgaria.(77) This opinion was later restated and elaborated upon by a number of Bulgarian scholars,(78) some of whom concluded that the educational part of the missionary work was the one that left an impact on Bulgarian society at the expense of the purely religious aspect of that work.(79)

The educational work of American missionaries was thus generally accepted and well regarded in the eyes of the natives. This was one kind of missionary activity which the Bulgarians had truly asked the Americans to engage in. Not surprisingly, this work was appreciated by many Bulgarians to a degree which might even support a curious hypothesis presented by H. N. Brailsford: He suggests that had the missionaries confined themselves only to education work "they might have promoted a reformation from within."(80) As all similar theses, this one cannot be definitely tested; however, it serves as another indication of the great impact that American education left not only on the condition of Bulgarian education but also on scholarly literature of the subject.

List of References

1. T. L. Byington to Dr. R. Anderson, June 7, 1860, ABC 16.9, vol. 4.

2. T. L. Byington to R. Anderson, October 21, 1863, ABC 16.9, vol. 4.

3. Ibid.

4. T. L Byington, "The Sixth Annual Report of the Eski Zagra Station," ABC 16.9, vol. 4.

5. J. F. Clarke, "10th Annual Report of Philippopolis Station, 1868-9." Clarke Papers.

6. N. G. Clark to J. F. Clarke, July 5, 1871, Clarke Papers.

7. H. E. Cole to J. L. Barton, November 29, 1899, ABC 16.9, vol. 12.

8. J. F. Clarke to Dr. Anderson, June 21, 1861, ABC 16.9, vol. 4.

9. W. W. Meriam to R. Anderson, February 20, 1861, ABC 16.9, vol. 4.

10. J. W. Baird to Sec. Clark, November 26, 1873, ABC 16.9, vol. 5.

11. J. W. Baird to sec. Clark, February 18, 1874, ABC 16.9, vol. 5.

12. For a detailed study of Catholic propaganda among the Bulgarians, see Kiril patriarkh bŭlgarski, *Katolicheskata propaganda sred bŭlgarite prez vtorata polovina na XIX v.*, (Sofia, 1962).

13. J. F. Clarke, *Sketch of the European Turkey Mission of the American Board,* (Boston: American Board of Commissioners for Foreign Missions, 1901), p. 4.

14. Atanas Iliev, *Spomeni*, (Sofia, 1926), pp. 33, 57.

15. Zhecho Atanasov, *Istoriia na bŭlgarskoto obrazovanie*, 2nd ed., (Sofia, 1974), p. 136.

16. *Istoriia na obrazovaniteto i pedagogicheskata misŭl v Bulgariia*, vol. 1, (Sofia, 1975), p. 207.

17. T. L. Byington to Dr. R. Anderson, July 15, 1861, ABC 16.9, vol. 4.

18. T. L. Byington to Dr. R. Anderson, July 29, 1862, ABC 16.9, vol. 4.

19. C. Hamlin, O. Winchester, T. C. Trowbridge, "Report of Committee on Bulgarian Schools," ABC 16.9, vol. 4.

20. T. L. Byington to Dr. Anderson, September 13, 1864, ABC 16.9, vol. 4.

21. J. F. Clarke to Dr. Anderson, June 8, 1865, ABC 16.9, vol. 4.

22. J. F. Clarke to N. G. Clark, (draft of a letter, sent February 26, 1869), Clarke Papers.

23. J. W. Baird to Sec. Clark, February 15, 1873, ABC 16.9, vol. 5.

24. G. D. Marsh to N. G. Clark, September 28, 1882, ABC 16.9, vol. 9, part 1.

25. W. E. Locke to N. G. Clark, February 27, 1891, ABC 16.9, vol. 13.

26. See Annual Tabular View for 1891 and subsequent years, ABC 16.9, vols. 11, 15.

27. W. W. Meriam, "3rd Annual Report of the Philippopolis Station," Clarke Papers.

28. H. C. Haskell to Dr. N. G. Clark, December 28, 1868, Clarke Papers.

29. "Minutes of the Convention of Missionaries to the Bulgarians, held in Philippopolis, March 1869," ABC 16.9 vol. 4; Henry C. Haskell, "11th Annual Report of the Philippopolis Station, 1869-70," Clarke Papers.

30. "Collegiate and Theological Institute," *Missionary News from Bulgaria* 3:1.

31. W. H. Belden, "Report for 1880-81 of the American Collegiate and Theological Institute," ABC 16.9, vol. 7.

32. See, for example, Hall, pp. 88-94, 191-200.

33. W. E. Locke to N. G. Clark, May 8, 1878, ABC 16.9, vol. 6.

34. *Missionary News from Bulgaria* 13:6, "The European Turkey Mission," *Missionary News from Bulgaria* 23:2.

35. *Amerikanskata kolegii͡a v gr. Samokov*, (Samokov: Pechatnit͡sa pri Amerikanskite gimnazii, n.d.), p. 3.

36. L. F. Ostrander, *Amerikanskoto nauchno bogoslovsko zavedenie v Samokov*, (Samokov: Evangelsko-Uchilishtna Pechatnit͡sa, n. d.), pp. 2-3.

37. H. C. Haskell, "Historical Sketch of the European Turkey Mission for its first 50 years," ABC 16.9, vol. 16.

38. T. L Byington, "The Fourth Annual Report of the Eski Zagra Station," ABC 16.9, vol. 4; "A Plan of the Female Boarding School at Eski Zagra," ABC 16.9, vol. 4.

39. H. P. Page, "Report of Samokov Station 1871-1872," Clarke Papers.

40. "The A. S. G. of Yesterday," *Samokov News* 1 (January, 1923): 3.

41. E. T. Maltbie, "Report of Girls' Mission School Samokov Bulgaria," /1902-1903/, ABC 16.9, vol. 16.

42. *Amerikanskata kolegii͡a*, p. 3.

43. E. M. Stone, "Girls' Boarding School at Samokov. Annual Report for 1880-1881," ABC 16.9, vol. 7.

44. Mary M. Haskell, "Annual Report of the American Girl's Boarding School, Samokov, Bulgaria, 1892-93," ABC 16.9, vol. 10.

45. H. C. Haskell, "Historical Sketch," ABC 16.9, vol. 16. For more information about the school see references from endnote 32 in this chapter.

46. J. W. Baird, "Report of Monastir Station for the year ending March 31st, 1882," Clarke Papers.

47. Harriet L. Cole, "Report of the Monastir Girls' Boarding School, for 1898-1899," Clarke Papers.

48. H. C. Haskell, "Historical Sketch," ABC 16.9, vol. 16.

49. T. T. Holway, "Annual Report of the Salonica Station for the Year from April 13, 1903-April 4, 1904," ABC 16.9, vol. 16; *The Thessalonica Agricultural and Industrial Institute for the Christian Industrial Training of Macedonian Boys. Annual Report, 1909*, (Thessalonica, 1910), p. 8.

50. *The Thessalonica*, pp. 11, 16-18.

51. Ibid., p. 19; W. C. Cooper, "Report of Salonica Station (Apr. 20, 1911-Apr. 1, 1912)," Clarke Papers.

52. Elizabeth C. Clarke, "Introductory Report of the Samokov Kindergarten," ABC 16.9, vol. 16.

53. E. C. Clarke, "Report of the Sofia Kindergarten for the year 1900-1901," ABC 16.9, vol. 16; E. C. Clarke, "Report of the Kindergarten Work in Sofia for the year 1908-09," ABC 16.9, vol. 16. The enrollment figures given by W. W. Hall are much higher; however, his source of information is not as direct as E. C. Clarke's report. See, Hall, p. 186.

54. Hall, p. 186.

55. G. D. Marsh to M. L. Barton, May 19, 1898, ABC 16.9, vol. 14.

56. Cited in Vatralski, p. 365.

57. Haskell, *American Influence*, p. 5.

58. /Paul Rowland/, *The Samokov American Schools. Sixty Years of Service in Bulgaria*, (Boston, 1924), p. 9.

59. Ibid., pp. 10-12.

60. George D. Marsh, "Report of the Philippopolis Station for the year ending April 2, 1912," Haskell Papers.

61. William Owen Carver, *The Course of Christian Missions. A History and an Interpretation*, (New York, Chicago, London and Edinborgh: Fleming H. Revell Company, n.d.), p. 225.

62. Henry M. Field, *The Greek Islands and Turkey after the War*, (New York: Charles Schriber's Sons, 1902), p. 162.

63. A. S. T͡sanov, "D-r I. F. Klark," *Zornit͡sa* (Plovdiv), July 13, 1916, p. 2.

64. W. W. Sleeper, "Report of the Trustees of the Collegiate and Theological Institute of Samokov, 1883-4," ABC 16.9, vol. 7.

65. W. W. Sleeper, "Report of the Trustees of the Collegiate and Theological Institute of Samokov for the year ending July 6, 1883," ABC 16.9, vol. 7; K. J. Tarzieff,

"Examination of the American Schools in Samokov," *Missionary News from Bulgaria* 19:2; "Geology and Mineralogy," *Missionary News from Bulgaria* 55:16.

66. J. W. Baird to N. G. Clark, November 16, 1883, ABC 16.9, vol. 7.

67. J. W. Baird to N. G. Clark, June 11, 1888, ABC 16.9, vol. 7.

68. Mother /M. M. Haskell/ to Edward B. Haskell, May 24, 1889, Haskell Papers.

69. H. C. Haskell, "Quarterly Report of the Samokov Station of the Eu. T. Mission for September 30th, 1896," ABC 16.9, vol. 10.

70. Mary L. Matthews to N. G. Clarke (sic), November 16, 1892, ABC 16.9, vol. 14.

71. H. C. Haskell, "Sec. Quar. Report of Samokov Station Aug.-Oct. 1894," ABC 16.9, vol. 10.

72. Copy of a letter received April 11th by Samokov Station, /1902/, ABC 16.9, vol. 15.

73. Stephen Momchiloff, "Report of the Teachers' Body of the Samokov C. and T. I.," ABC 16.9, vol. 16.

74. Ibid.

75. Cited in /Paul Rowland/, *The Samokov American Schools*, p. 7.

76. Ikonomov, p. 79.

77. Iv. D. Shishmanov, "Novi danni za istorii͡ata na nasheto vŭzrazhdane," *Bulgarski pregled* (Sofia) 4 (February, 1898): 54.

78. See for example, Veselin Traikov, "Protestantskite misioneri i borbata na bŭlgarskii͡a narod za tsŭrkovna svoboda," *Bŭlgarii͡a v sveta ot drevnostta do nashi dni*, vol. 1, (Sofia, 1979), p. 466; *Istorii͡a na obrazovanieto*, p. 254.

79. Vel. Iordanov, "Uchastieto na Amerika v nasheto vŭzrazhdane," *Uchilishten pregled* (Sofia) 35 (September, 1936): 933.

80. Brailsford, p. 74.

CHAPTER III
LITERARY AND OTHER ACTIVITIES

1. *Missionary Literature and the Bulgarians*

Initially, American missionary involvement among the Bulgarians was to a great extent a direct response to the avid desire of the natives to have Christian literature. As shown earlier*, the Bulgarian population was willing to buy missionary texts written in its own vernacular. In the words of J. F. Clarke from a later account of the mission's work in European Turkey:

> The destruction of books in their language by the Greeks led Bulgarians to purchase eagerly the New Testament, first published in 1856, chiefly because it was in the sweet mother tongue. . .(1)

Profiting from years of experience, Clarke was able to point out the reason behind Bulgarian willingness to buy missionary literature. The circumstances surrounding the Bulgarian Revival were such that, at first, any literature in the spoken language was extremely difficult to prepare and to disseminate. At that opportune moment, the Americans were able to offer at least some books which, in effect, fed the already existing demand for literature. For example, in 1859, Charles F. Morse, the missionary residing at Adrianople, reported the Bulgarian eagerness "with which they welcome our tracts," coupled with the fact that "four or five editions of the Testament. . .have already been circulated among the people." These occurrences, according to Morse, underscored the necessity to occupy all important centers in the field.(2)

At this early stage of the missionary work among the Bulgarians, the promise of influencing a willing population seemed realistic. Soon, however, the missionaries noticed that while the desire for literature continued to exist, Protestantism

* See page 6.

did not increase its following in the lands south of the Balkan Mountains. In 1860, T. L. Byington observed that the purchase of Bibles was not a symptom of interest in Protestant Christianity for the majority of the natives. Regarding the distribution of such materials, he wrote from Eski Zagra:

> That many purchase because of their desire to read the Bible is doubtless true, but I think it was evident that the majority purchased because it was the cheapest reading book they could find for their children.(3)

The Americans were quickly aware of such monetary considerations among the Bulgarians; nevertheless, they continued to supply religious texts, the sale of which at least at first looked quite promising. In the early 1860's, a missionary bookstore was opened in Philippopolis and then temporarily closed after a leading Bulgarian publishing and bookselling firm agreed to distribute missionary literature throughout the entire country*.(4) This step clearly illustrates that prominent Bulgarians also appreciated the apparent attractiveness the the missionary books held for the general population.

In the mid-1860's, the Americans continued to report a lively interest in their literature. Following a visit in the town of Kalofer, J. F. Clarke wrote that the missionary books had created among the local population a favorable disposition toward Protestantism; he added, however, his fear that "there are no hearts earnestly seeking to know of Christ."(5) At the village of Peshtera, Clarke even found that the missionaries were considered friends because they were supplying the natives with books in their own language in contrast to the Greek priests who were forcing Greek religious texts on the Bulgarians.(6) At a time of particularly sharp conflicts in the movement for religious independence, the local people certainly welcomed missionary-printed materials which, in fact, aided that movement.

The favorable response that American missionary literature generated did not conceal the apparent lack of religious impact on that very population which was eagerly

* The firm was the famous "Khr. Danov i s-ie" /Khristo Danov and co./ which signed a contract with the missionaries in Philippopolis in April 1862. The document is part of the Clarke Papers.

seeking the Christian writings. The representatives of the American Board were faced with a most disturbing situation. The Bulgarian appetite for books did not diminish, but the same was true of their indifference to the Protestant message. What once was taken to mean a desire for Protestantism now could be regarded only as a desire for books in the native language. Clarke himself explained this to his superiors in Boston, concluding that the initial missionary hopes for quick results in the Bulgarian field were not well founded. The Bulgarians' desire "to posses (sic) the Sacred Scriptures... caused many to suppose that the Bulgarians were seeking the religion of the gospel. . .but it has never, to any extent, been true."(7) They simply wanted to have books.

Atanas Iliev, a native of Eski Zagra, described in his memoirs his own infatuation with Protestantism and the missionary publications. During the 1860's, Iliev was reading all available Protestant literature, an endeavor which his father did not oppose. Eventually, in 1866-1867, his interests moved to books of a patriotic and scientific nature, and he no longer had any use for the missionary materials.(8) This example of a Bulgarian's attitude toward the readings supplied by the American Board coincides with the missionaries' impressions. The Americans were able to detect that, similar to other means of evangelical work, the dissemination of literature in Bulgarian was valued on its own terms and not because of its Protestant content. The Bulgarian people, in their general effort to emancipate themselves, would not be satisfied simply by one type of literature. Their needs were much more complex and could not be adequately met by the missionaries.

However, with the gradual improvement of literary life in Bulgaria, especially following the creation of the Principality in 1878, the demand for missionary literature continued. At that time, though, the Bulgarians openly admitted that the relative inexpensiveness of these publications was the one factor that made them attractive. This was true particularly of the outspoken opponents of Protestantism, who in this manner explained the continuing flow of missionary literature. A Philippopolis-based journal, for example, cited the inexpensiveness of the evangelical newspaper to explain its relative success throughout the country.(9) A historian of the

Bulgarian church, on the other hand, found it necessary to remark that "the literate Bulgarians did read and are reading (missionary literature) with a particular pleasure because it is quite inexpensive and is sometimes given away."(10) As evidence of active missionary involvement in Bulgarian publishing, these statements were dated 1887 and 1907, respectively.

While Bulgarians in their own state would tend to denigrate the role of missionary literature in such a manner, those who remained under Turkish rule had a much greater appreciation for American publications in Bulgarian. A Bulgarian teacher in Macedonia, for example, expressed his gratitude to one of the native missionary helpers:

> You have saved Macedonia from falling into the hands of the Greeks, because, by your circulation of the Tract Primer and other Bulgarian books which otherwise they could not have obtained, you have enabled our children to study their mother tongue.(11)

The Protestant aspect of missionary literary activities was completely ignored, but the books themselves were regarded as crucial to the preservation of the national awareness of these Bulgarians. Circumstances surrounding the Revival created a definite trend toward native acceptance of the foreigners and their work. Quite the same as in the area of education, the Bulgarians welcomed only the non-Protestant aspects of missionary endeavors. The Americans, on the other hand, were pursuing many tasks which were not purely evangelical in hopes that such methods would accomplish their ultimate goal. This is the real substance behind the assertion that the Bulgarian Revival made possible the very existence of the American mission.*

At the beginning of the American Board's involvement in European Turkey, one of the missionaries proclaimed that "the Bulgarians have as yet but few books. There seems to be a most promising field for the working of a Sanctified press among this people."(12) To a certain extent, these words proved to be prophetic. The field for publishing activities remained promising indeed. The native attitude toward Protestant literature definitely indicates its acceptance and

* See page 77

influence in Bulgarian society. The role of that literature, however, did not really fulfill the missionary expectations for speedy conversion of the Orthodox population. Instead, it fulfilled to a much greater degree the Bulgarian need for books in the spoken language.

2. *Missionary Publishing and Literary Work for the Bulgarians*

The missionaries of the American Board in European Turkey engaged in different kinds of activities in order to prepare and distribute appropriate printed materials. These included translating, writing occasional original works, and publishing and circulating the end-products. Perhaps the best expressions of the significance of that aspect of missionary work is the data represented in Table 3. Year after year, the Americans produced a significant quantity of printed material. The available information for thirty-three years (1870-1871, 1873-1874, 1878-1895, 1897-1905, 1907-1909) shows that the printing facilities used by the missionaries averaged approximately 2,201,608 pages a year, thus producing an almost astronomical number of pages during the recorded period—72,653,077. According to missionary calculations, the Bulgarian population was 4,551,000, indicating that by 1909 the Americans had managed to supply an average of more than 16 pages* of missionary printed material for every Bulgarian man, woman, and child. These figures, of course, represent the ideal situation in terms of distribution; the actual circulation of such materials is not well-documented. Nevertheless, the great volume of missionary literature in Bulgarian is indicative of the emphasis placed on such activities.

The publishing work of the European Turkey Mission was at first concentrated in Constantinople where it was maintained until the beginning of 1898. Following that year, missionary publications came out primarily in Samokov. At that location, an "Evangelical School Press" was opened at the Institute in 1884, and eventually it was able to satisfy most of the missionary needs.(13)

* It is not clear how much more the actual figure is than 16 pages since information for some years is not available.

TABLE 3*

STATISTICAL RESULTS: PUBLICATION (1870-1909)

YEAR	NUMBER of PAGES
1870	5,018,000
1871	777,000
1873	752,000
1874	522,000
1878	2,462,500
1879	1,498,624
1880	5,179,424
1881	3,331,588
1882	5,009,100
1883	3,378,848
1884	3,627,080
1885	1,165,016
1886	2,886,272
1887	2,017,968
1888	1,816,044
1889	1,445,612
1890	1,543,300
1891	1,186,360
1893	2,950,336
1894	1,221,224
1895	1,199,904
1897	2,260,000
1898	520,607
1899	840,634
1900	1,030,438
1901	811,588
1902	ca. 900,000
1903	ca. 700,000
1904	806,650
1905	1,620,890
1907	2,548,516
1908	2,113,214
1909	9,519,340

*All the information compiled in Table 3 may be found in ABC 16.9, vols. 5, 7, 11, 15.

The focus of missionary publication was Christian literature. The American Board took an active part in the work of preparing a complete edition of the Bible in the vernacular. In the person of Elias Riggs, the European Turkey Mission found a great linguist in addition to a prominent missionary. Riggs, in cooperation with leading Bulgarian literary figures, directed the translation and revision of the Old and New Testaments into Bulgarian. In 1871, the complete Bible was published*, and together with the actual founding of the European Turkey Mission, this represented one of the high points in the American Board's involvement with the Bulgarian population.(14) Elias Riggs continued his scholarly work and was able to produce two other monumental projects, which were completed in the late 1890s: one was a New Testament Commentary in two volumes, the other a Biblical Dictionary.(15) Finally, among his numerous translations, one more compact work should be mentioned. In 1907, a revised edition of hymns in Bulgarian was published by the missionaries. It contained 626 hymns, 479 of which were translated by Riggs.(16)

Religious and moralistic tracts were widely used by the missionaries in their work. The variety was great, and they published numerous copies. By 1896, for example, the European Turkey Mission reported a total of almost seventy tracts issued, each in quantities of 5,000 copies.(17) Often these would be distributed free of charge. The extent of the Mission's free circulation of printed materials may be illustrated by the example of missionary advertising in 1888 and 1889. At that time, the Americans were offering eighty titles in their bookstores for sale and seventy-six titles free of charge.(18) Whether this practice was caused by a desire to make Protestant literature more accessible or was due to difficulties in distribution is not clear. There are indications, however, that at least on one occasion the missionaries were forced to reduce the prices of their publications and to sell some as old paper due to a lack of reader interest. In 1902, for

* The financial cost of this endeavor was covered by the British and Foreign Bible Society. It should be added that the European Turkey Mission was in active cooperation for the distribution of Christian literature in Bulgarian with the above and other (mostly American) Bible and tract societies.

This aspect of mission work is not studied here.

instance, they sold some 4,000,000 pages of printed material as waste paper.(19)

Perhaps the most widely acceptable literature consisted of translations of textbooks and other learning aids which were prepared by the missionaries themselves. The first two foreign grammars of the Bulgarian language were the product of American missionaries. Elias Riggs prepared a twenty-four page booklet, *Notes on the Grammar of the Bulgarian Language*, which was published in Smyrna in 1844. This pioneering work was followed by a book authored by Charles F. Morse, *A Grammar of the Bulgarian language with exercises and English and Bulgarian vocabularies*, published in Constantinople in 1859. The next year a second work prepared by Morse came out, this time an English-Bulgarian and Bulgarian-English dictionary, again printed in Constantinople.(20) Initially, these publications primarily served the needs of the missionaries, but the latter proved quite useful in the missionary schools as well.

Many Bulgarian schools during the 1860's made regular use of American translations of standard textbooks which were originally done by missionaries and native workers to satisfy the needs of the first missionary schools. Examples of such books are a *Tract Primer*, a translation of Calvin Cutter's *First Book of Anatomy, Physiology and Hygiene*, Benjamin Greenleaf's *Algebra*, and Daniel Olmstead's *School Philosophy*. Cutter's and Greenleaf's textbooks were published by and at the expense of the above mentioned Bulgarian bookfirm of Khristo G. Danov.(21) The Bulgarian schools also used other "non-controversial" Protestant books, particularly in the early to mid-1860s; however, by the end of the decade, missionary books were excluded from the native schools due to the stigma attached to such publications.(22) The textbooks published by the Bulgarian company were not regarded as Protestant books and continued to be in demand.

The Americans continued to translate textbooks for the needs of their schools during the next decades. The Bulgarian Evangelical Society published a translation of Mark Hopkins' *Mental Philosophy* prepared by the missionary J. H. House in 1886.(23) Dr. Kingsbury, on his part, did two translations and had them published at the mission press in Samokov in the early 1890s. In their order of appearance the textbooks were:

Thomas H. Huxley's *Physiology* and Charles A. Young's *Astronomy*.(24) The last work was intended for use in the national schools as well due to the lack of any other textbooks on the subject. In addition, the teachers at the Samokov Institute prepared a manual for the study of English.(25)

These titles, combined with the works which appeared in the 1860s, exhaust the nonreligious literary endeavors of the European Turkey Mission. With the passing of time, the missionaries no longer* involved themselves in such activities. When their work began, the needs of Bulgarian society were such that any foreign help in the area of publishing was welcome. By the 1890s, however, when missionary translations of textbooks last appeared, native cultural development had largely made such work unnecessary.

The Americans were much more persistent and successful in a different literary field. Their efforts to issue periodicals in Bulgarian resulted in the publication of two different newspapers, both bearing the name, *Zornit͡sa* (Morning Star). The original start of an evangelical newspaper in Bulgarian was the work of a Methodist colleague of the missionaries in European Turkey. In 1864, Dr. Albert Long began his monthly paper, *Zornit͡sa*, in Constantinople. Long's periodical continued to come out until 1871. In 1872, the European Turkey Mission, at its Second Annual Meeting, voted to ask Elias Riggs to take over the editorship of *Zornit͡sa* as soon as his other duties allowed.(26) The monthly periodical was reissued in 1874, and at the same time, a decision was approved for the publication of a weekly evangelical paper.(27) The first issues of the weekly *Zornit͡sa* came out in December of 1875, but 1876 is considered the year of its inception. The editor of the weekly was Theodore L. Byington who also took over the editorship of the monthly in 1880. The two *Zornit͡sas* differed not only in the frequency of their publication, but also in content. The

* One exception to this related to the events of 1908 when the Mission briefly considered the idea of publishing an English-Bulgarian Dictionary. A Bulgarian publishing company engaged in similar work wrote a letter of protest to the American Board in Boston, complaining of unfair competition in regard to these missionary plans. The letter included the following statement: "making and publishing grammars and dictionaries is not in the sphere of missionary activities." (See, "Globus" to the Secretary of the American Missionary Board, May 29, 1908, Clarke Papers). The idea was soon dropped.

monthly became the children's paper of the Mission while the weekly addressed the adult population.

The two periodicals were published, like Long's paper, in Constantinople. They survived many years of great change in Turkey and Bulgaria without interruption. The one major change came in 1885 when a new editor took over management of the newspapers; he was a Scotsman by the name of Robert Thomson in the service of the American Board. The weekly had to be stopped at the end of 1896 due to financial difficulties and was renewed in the beginning of 1902 with a Bulgarian editor, A. S. T͡sanov. It was published in Philippopolis.(28) The children's paper was combined with another missionary periodical* at the beginning of 1896. In the process, it acquired a new editor, F. L. Kingsbury, and the paper started to come out bimonthly. It was discontinued in 1901 when the sum of money used for its publication was transferred to fund the weekly *Zorni͡tsa*.(29)

The weekly *Zorni͡tsa* was always regarded as one of the best results of missionary involvement in Bulgaria. From its beginning, the Americans reported that the paper was favorably received in "the leading places" of the field.(30) Famous Bulgarian literary figures approved of it. Li͡uben Karavelov, for example, wrote that the language and style of *Zorni͡tsa* was superior to that of other Bulgarian periodicals with the exception of *Gaida*, which was edited by Petko R. Slaveikov*.(31) Slaveikov himself appreciated *Zorni͡tsa* enough to allow the reprinting of some of its articles on the pages of another famous newspaper that he edited, *Makedonii͡a*.(32)

The positive reaction that missionary periodicals generally created among the native literate population may be best shown by referring to Table 4 where all available information

* From January, 1887 to 1896 the so-called *Detevoditel* (Children's Guide) was published in Samokov by Dr. F. L. Kingsbury. This monthly paper had a list of 600 subscribers in the early 1890's. *See Missionary News from Bulgaria* 11:4; Edward B. Haskell, *Points Picked from the Annual Meeting of the European Turkey Mission, Samokov, Bulgaria Apr. 12-19, 1892*, (Samokov: Industrial Dept. Press, n.d.), p. 1.

* Slaveikov was one of the Bulgarians who worked with Elias Riggs on the translation of the New Testament into Bulgarian. As one of the top literary and political figures in the period of the National Revival, his connection and tolerance of the American Protestants brought him many unpleasant accusations by his compatriots. See, M. Stoi͡anov, "Petko R., Slaveikov i protestantskata propaganda u nas," *Rodina* (Sofia) 3 (March 1941): 90-98.

TABLE 4*

STATISTICAL RESULTS: ZORNITSA (1874-1908)

YEAR	MONTHLY ZORNITSA		WEEKLY ZORNITSA	
	COPIES	SUBSCRIBERS	COPIES	SUBSCRIBERS
1874	2,000	2,000		
1877[a]		900		3,000
1878	1,050		1,540	
1879		2,200		2,900
1880		3,700		3,750
1881	4,708		4,022	
1883	5,382		3,634	
1884	4,666		3,372	
1885	4,817		3,350	3,100
1886	3,990		4,669	4,260
1887	3,566		4,084	
1888	3,400		4,287	3,700
1889	2,200		2,999	
1890	1,870	1,680	1,925	1,505
1891	1,990	1,778	1,826	1,494
1892	2,172		1,732	
1893	1,948	1,600	1,554	1,300
1894	1,604		1,586	
1895	1,366[b]		1,468	
1896			1,176[c]	
1903				880
1904				940
1905				ca. 1,000
1906				1,300
1907				ca. 1,300
1908				1,364

*All the information compiled in Table 4 may be found in ABC 16.9, vols. 7, 10, 16.

[a]For year ending May 1.

[b]Transferred to Samokov and combined with Detevoditel. Discontinued in 1901.

[c]Discontinued from the end of the year to January 1, 1902.

regarding the printing and number of subscribers of the two *Zornitsas* is printed. The distribution of the newspapers was unprecedented for the Bulgarian press at that time. Constantinople, for instance, was the publication site for twenty-one Bulgarian newspapers, including the two *Zornitsas*, prior to the Russo-Turkish War of 1877-1878. The native periodicals could boast at most 900-1,000 subscribers.(33) But by May 1, 1877, the two *Zornitsas* had a combined circulation of 3,900 which clearly put them ahead of all Bulgarian newspapers. According to missionary information, that distribution lead was maintaned by the Protestant papers until 1890.(34) The data in Table 4 indicated that circulation peaked in the 1880s. The jump in the number of subscribers from 1885 to 1886 was explained by martial law in Bulgaria following the unification with Eastern Rumelia when the government severely restricted the issuing of Bulgarian newspapers.(35) The years that followed witnessed the irreversible decline in popularity of the paper, ending with the five-year interruption of 1897-1901. The comeback of the weekly, starting in 1902, was very unimpressive in quantity, but at least it experienced some growth thereafter. It should be remembered that the move from Constantinople to Philippopolis meant a loss of Bulgarian subscribers in Macedonia and Thrace who could not be easily reached by a periodical originating from the Bulgarian Principality.

In 1894, when it was becoming evident that the newspapers were steadily declining in circulation and losing the competition with the native press, one of the American missionaries wisely remarked: "I regard the falling off in the circulation of the *Zornitsa* as a permanent thing. It is not for us to complain that others publish but shout with joy."(36) Certainly, the missionaries could not hope to supersede all the Bulgarian newspapers once political independence allowed free cultural and intellectual development.

The accomplishments of the periodicals were such that even their gradual decline did not diminish their importance. For the Americans, *Zornitsa* in its two formats was the most effective means of communication with the native population. In 1919, Edward Haskell summarized the role of the periodicals, especially the weekly:

> While treating all subjects from an evangelical Christian standpoint it never was sectarian, and avoided attacks on the Orthodox Church. It thus entered hundreds of villages never visited by a preacher and was valued by a multitude of Orthodox readers.(37)

Another missionary, George Marsh, considered the weekly *Zornit͡sa* the most effective means of influencing the Bulgarians. His opinion was that "no branch of. .Mission work is doing better service as an evangelizing agency than this 'Morning Star'."(38) Perhaps if one must judge the European Turkey Mission on the relative success of its different activities, its accomplishments as the publisher of Bulgarian periodicals might be placed at the top of the list.

The success of the *Zornit͡sa*s was significant from the Bulgarian perspective as well. Travellers visiting the country noted that even Orthodox priests aided the circulation of the papers.(39) The respectability of the weekly was such that at the time of the Russo-Turkish War of 1877-1878, Bulgarian monks on Mount Athos subscribed for several copies.(40) Another indication of its popularity among the readers is the fact that in some regions of Macedonia the name of the Protestant periodical became a generic term meaning "newspaper."(41) Such a transformation could only be explained by an awareness among the Bulgarians in this part of the Ottoman Empire that *Zornit͡sa* was their first and best known newspaper.

The clearest sign of the newspapers' acceptance in Bulgarian society, however, remains their long lists of subscribers. While the figures are impressive by themselves, the actual number of readers was far greater. If a household received a newspaper, this meant that relatives and neighbors read it, too. If a reading room or school subscribed, as was practiced in those days, the number of actual readers increased even more dramatically.

In general, the literary and publication activities of the American Board for the Bulgarians, much like their educational efforts, remained permanently a feature of the history of the Bulgarian cultural revival. The already quoted observation by George Marsh regarding the role of education (see page 72) was fully meant for the importance of the missionary publication work in Bulgaria. Education and publication were the two closely related missionary endeavors that determined the reputation and influence of the American Board in the region.*

The role of the literary activities of the European Turkey Mission in the cultural advancement of the Bulgarian nation is readily acknowledged by historians dealing with this subject. Reflecting the surprising uniformity of opinion existing not only among contemporaries but also among subsequent researchers in the field, one Bulgarian historian observed that by "translating the Bible into the vernacular Bulgarian, publishing various literature, the Protestants responded. . .to the need for literature and books, which did not exist in a sufficient degree in our enslaved country."(42)

It is difficult to determine how the literary endeavors of the American missionaries affected the fulfillment of their task to evangelize the native population. One point is clear, however: the preparation and publishing of books and other literature in Bulgarian was important to both the missionary comprehension of their role in European Turkey and the cultural growth of Bulgarian society.

3. *Philanthropy*

The period of missionary involvement among the Bulgarian population brought many changes to the people inhabiting the Balkan Peninsula. These were times of economic growth as well as political and cultural advances—but also times of great crises, violence, and bloodshed. In spite of all the difficulties accompanying their work, the Americans never left the field or interrupted their activities. They even often involved themselves in humanitarian work aimed at relieving the frequent periods of

* In illustrating the influence of the American Board in Bulgaria, Grabill claims that seventy-five of the first one hundred books in modern Bulgarian were printed by the Board's press. However, he neglects to give his source of information, which makes it impossible to verify the statement. It should be kept in mind that according to a leading Bulgarian scholar, there were 1,560 Bulgarian books published in the period of 1843-1877 (see N. Nachov, "Novobŭlgarskata kniga i pechatnoto delo u nas ot 1806 do 1877 god.," *Sbornik na Bŭlgarskata akademii͡a na naukite* 15:23). While not directly refuting Grabill's statement, this information makes his assertion highly improbable.

great human suffering brought about by wars, political unrest, and uprisings. While these missionary engagements were not directed at the Bulgarians exclusively, events still unfolded in such a manner in the area that the Bulgarians were the ones who most often needed aid. Typically, the missionaries did not hesitate to offer their services whenever they perceived an area where their involvement would be appreciated and, perhaps more importantly, needed.

The first instance when the Americans engaged in purely philanthropic activities was related to the ill-fated Bulgarian Uprising of 1876 which was followed by the so called "Bulgarian massacres." The Americans were in a position to acquire first hand information about the extent of civilian suffering* and to ask for outside help. Following an exploratory tour in September 1876, Rev. J. F. Clarke wrote a letter to Secretary N. G. Clark in Boston asking for aid for the suffering Bulgarians. The missionaries did not seek aid from the American Board specifically but from the American public in general.(43)

During the same time, Clarke was actively involved as a coordinator and distributor of aid for the suffering in the district of Philippopolis. He was working under the direction of a Constantinople-based Central Committee for the Relief of Distress in Bulgaria and c.** and entrusted with the actual distribution of food, clothing, and other necessary articles. Clarke was the chief supervisor of fourteen native men who acted as agents of the Central Committee in the region. Among Clarke's accomplishments in philanthropy were the following: the erection of hospitals in the villages of Batak and Radulovo, which were also used as soup kitchens; the distribution of blankets and clothing; the distribution of 10,911 kg of grain to 9,370 families; and the purchase and distribution of 440 oxen amongst 22 villages.(44)

Another missionary, G. D. Marsh, worked for a time distributing aid on behalf of the Central Committee. He was involved in the distribution of flour to 120 families in the city

* More on this subject is available in James F. Clarke, "Reporting the Bulgarian Massacres: 'The suffering in Bulgaria,' by Henry O. Dwight and the Rev. J. F. Clarke (1876)," *Southeastern Europe/L'Europe du Sud-Est* 4, part 2 (1977), pp. 278-296.

**The organization was formed in September with the task of collecting and distributing aid from Europe and America.

of Îambol, in assisting people in the reconstruction of their houses by supplying them with tools, and in distributing 72 oxen and 30 plows in the village of Boîadzhik.(45)

Clarke worked on behalf of other philanthropists interested in Bulgaria. He collected needed information for Lady Strangford who was engaged in relief activities in the region of Philippopolis. He distributed her funds and, in addition, the European Turkey Mission supplied Lady Strangford with translators (from among the students in the Samokov schools) who worked with a medical team of six nurses and five doctors from England.(46)

The philanthropic activities of the missionaries were not always completely separate from their religious mission, however. At one point in Clarke's relief work, the American Consul-General in Constantinople, Eugene Schuyler, voiced complaints on behalf of the Bulgarians that the missionary was attempting "to proselytise them" in the hospital at Batak.(47) Apparently, Clarke was reading the Bible and praying in that hospital, acts which offended the natives. The missionary defended himself by pointing out that the bishop in Philippopolis had approved of prayer in the hospital. In fact, Clarke proceeded to call to the hospital the village priest who had received a blanket from the Central Committee and who "was ready cordially to join the service."(48) This particular missionary did not think it improper to mix philantropy with Protestantism. Such behavior was not inappropriate, in fact, since Clarke was first a missionary and then a humanitarian worker.

In spite of isolated cases of conflict between the missionaries turned philanthropists and the Bulgarians, the native population certainly welcomed this episode in American Protestant involvement with them. Lady Strangford, during her visit to Panagîurishte, was told by the village leader, perhaps not without some insincerity, that the natives "have always been glad to see missionaries."(49) Naturally, one must cautiously interpret such reaction from those receiving the benefits of relief. It seems logical, however, that the Bulgarians were glad to see the missionaries as relief workers, if not as propagators of Protestantism in times of great deprivation.

The next critical period in Balkan history which offered the missionaries an opportunity to act as philanthropists was the Serbo-Bulgarian War of 1885 which followed the reuniting of the Principality with Eastern Rumelia. The European Turkey Mission was unable to carry out its plan to open a hospital for wounded soldiers. As a result, the missionaries engaged mainly in visiting the wounded and distributing tracts and copies of the New Testament and the weekly *Zornit͡sa*. The Minister of War in the Principality did not allow such activities in the army which limited American involvement only to the wounded.(50)

The Ilinden Uprising of 1903* and the subsequent wave of refugees into Bulgaria presented the missionaries with their last opportunity to extend humanitarian aid to the native population.** The Americans were again involved as distributors of aid that various American and British societies sent to them. In their report, three missionaries, J. F. Clarke, L. F. Ostrander and R. Thomson, stated that they had spent $5,405.70 to help 5,500 refugees from Macedonia.(51) In essence, this endeavor was what to a large extent occupied the Samokov Station from November 1903 through 1904. The Monastir Station, which happened to be in the center of revolutionary ferment, had its regular activities disrupted completely and mainly performed relief work. The missionaries helped 61,500 people by the end of March 1904.(52) They even opened an orphanage, using British donations for that purpose. The institution was known as the Essery Memorial Orphanage.(53)

The Philippopolis Station also did its share of relief work. Rev. G. D. Marsh and his wife spent several months (May-November 1904 and January-February, 1905) in the region of Adrianople where they administered the distribution of aid.(54)

* On August 2, 1903, which was St. Elijah's Day (or "Ilinden" in Bulgarian), an uprising broke out in the region of Bitola. This was followed by a revolt in the region of Adrianople on the Feast of the Transfiguration ("Preobrazhenie" in Bulgarian). The revolts were crushed by the end of October.

** J. F. Clarke worked as relief agent of a London-based organization for Armenian refugees in the area of Burgas during 1896. He was engaged in that capacity for 45 days. See J. F. Clarke, "Report of Philippopolis Station for year 1896-7," ABC 16.9, vol. 10.

In the course of this campaign, new conflicts developed between Americans and natives. The first arose when the pastor of the Sofia church, Marko N. Popov, became a special commissioner of the *Christian Herald,* a New York newspaper which collected a large amount of money for the Bulgarian refugees.(55) Some of the missionaries thought that a Bulgarian should not be entrusted with the funds, fearing that the money, in Bulgarian hands, might be used for revolutionary purposes.(56)

Another problem also arose with the Marshes who were distributing Bibles and New Testaments to the poor in their relief activities. The Bulgarian press claimed that the missionaries were introducing the element of religious propaganda in their humanitarian work.(57) It seems, indeed, that the representatives of the American Board had difficulty completely separating the evangelical element from their philanthropic deeds. One of the missionary women, Ellen R. Baird, at the time of the relief effort in 1903-1904 wrote the following illuminating statement: "The poorer classes receive our financial aid gladly, but do not care to accept our teaching except in theory."(58) She was obviously expecting that the acceptance of material aid would naturally bring about acceptance of Protestantism. Since this was hardly the case, Baird felt the need to include an expression of her disappointment in one of the official reports dealing with the work of the Samokov Station.

As a rule, the missionaries did not apply the above logic in their handling of relief. Nevertheless, the periodic use of proselytising methods while performing acts of philanthropy leaves the Americans open to criticism. In spite of these "lapses" in missionary zeal, however, the men and women sent by the American Board contributed a great deal toward the alleviation of much suffering during critical times in Bulgarian history. Once more, the missionaries demonstrated their sensitivity to the real and changing need of the people amongst whom they lived.

4. *Medical and Temperance Activities*

The arrival of Dr. F. L. Kingsbury in Samokov on May 13, 1881 marked the beginning of a seventeen-year missionary medical career for him in Bulgaria;(59) it also meant the establishment of a medical branch for the European Turkey Mission. This aspect of American missionary involvement among the Bulgarians was relatively short-lived and on a small scale. Nevertheless, it deserves some discussion.

Dr. Kingsbury received permission to practice medicine from the Bulgarian authorities by November 1882 and began his work as practitioner, serving mainly his co-workers and the students at the Samokov schools.(60) He was full of ideas for expanding his work which, however, did not materialize. For a time, he entertained plans to open a medical school and a children's hospital, but the approval of the American Board was not forthcoming.(61) At one time, in 1889, Kingsbury came very close to the realization of opening a hospital due to the bequest of a native Protestant. His heirs, however, disputed the legality of the will and, consequently, the hospital project never received a contribution from his estate.(62)

Following this disappointment, Kingsbury continued his regular practice. In 1891-1892, he reported to average forty-five patients a week and for the fifteen months beginning January 1897, he was able to treat some 2,271 patients.(63) Certainly, nothing exceptional or extraordinary could be detected in his achievements. Kingsbury's own dissatisfaction with the scope of his work was felt in his active involvement in the work of other branches of missionary activity. As mentioned earlier, he worked on the translations of two textbooks and on their publication; he also edited the mission children's paper for a while. In addition, the doctor made clear his opinion to Boston in a letter written at the beginning of 1893:

> In our mission, as conducted, I think little can be said in favor of Medical Missions. It amounts, in my opinion simply to having a doctor for the members of the mission and the schools.(64)

The unimpressive accounts of the medical mission in European Turkey were most likely due to the fact that in a country such as the Bulgarian Principality, medical expertise was available and even though many things in this area needed improvement, a missionary doctor was not a necessity for the Mission. Certainly, the Americans, not to mention the natives, managed without their own physician before Kingsbury's arrival. Not surprisingly, following his departure in May 1898, (65) no one from the Board questioned the end of the entire experiment of a medical mission in European Turkey.

The missionaries also pursued the cause of temperance among the native population. The whole idea of temperance was generally unknown in this part of the Balkan Peninsula. As one American wrote: "the idea of abstinence is wholly new ...intoxicating drinks are...considered to be decidedly beneficial, as renewing life, and health, and strength."(66) Much like the initiation of medical mission work in Bulgaria, the temperance efforts by the Americans were therefore uninvited. In fact, the original idea of beginning such efforts did not even come from the missionaries.

The first steps for the promotion of the temperance cause in Bulgaria came as a result of the intervention of the Worlds Woman's Christian Temperance Union centered in the United States. A member of this society asked Zoe A. M Locke, a missionary woman residing in Philippopolis, to lead the spread of temperance ideas in Bulgaria.(67) This occurred in the first half of 1887 and was followed by the quick organization of two temperance societies in Philippopolis—one for young men and one for women.(68)

The offer of another outsider led to a different form of temperance work in the early 1890s. By the suggestion of one Demorest from New York, contests among speakers using his temperance declamations were organized in the two Samokov schools. Fourteen such exercises were enacted between 1890 and 1892, the winners receiving silver and gold medals supplied by Demorest.(69)

Meanwhile, the temperance societies in the country met and formed a General Temperance Union in April 1892. By that time there were nine such organizations in Bulgaria. They were mostly an outgrowth of the evangelical communities and rarely included non-Protestant natives. Significantly, the organization of the Temperance Union took place in one of the centers of missionary activity, Samokov.(70) The society met annually in conjunction with the annual meetings of other evangelical organizations, such as the conferences. The societies that made up the membership of the Temperance Union gradually increased in number, totalling 16 by

1895.(71) However, the narrow character of the movement was not overcome that easily. Only in 1909, could the Union claim that it no longer represented only Protestant native communities.(72) The actual membership, however, had not been verified, leaving the above claim unsubstantiated.

Perhaps the most active among the missionaries in the sphere of temperance work was J. F. Clarke who devoted much of his time to the publishing and distribution of appropriate tracts, posters, and other materials. Using personal funds, donations from the United States, Britain, and other countries, Clarke was instrumental in the preparation of 532,200 such publications from 1896 to 1911. The distribution was greatly aided by the full cooperation of the Ministry of Education, the Exarchate, and the Foreign Ministry. The latter two circulated temperance materials for the Bulgarians in Turkey. In his old age, the missionary was able to develop very high political contacts due to his zeal on behalf of the temperance idea. Clarke received an audience with the Bulgarian queen, Eleonora, and even contributed to the opening of a discussion in the National Assembly about the possibility of prohibiting alcohol consumption in the country.(73)

Clarke's public campaign did not bring about any serious consideration of anti-alcohol legislation; nevertheless, the Bulgarian advocates of temperance certainly appreciated his efforts and dedication. In fact, he came to be known posthumously as the "first apostle of temperance in Bulgaria."(74)

List of References

1. J. F. Clarke, *Sketch*, p. 4.

2. C. F. Morse. "Annual Report of Adrianople Station," /2nd Annual Report of the *Bulgarian* Department of the Mission/, Clarke Papers.

3. T. L. Byington to Dr. R. Anderson, June 7, 1860, ABC 16.9, vol. 4.

4. W. W. Meriam, "3rd Annual Report of the Philippopolis Station," Clarke Papers.

5. J. F. Clarke to Dr. Anderson, March 4, 1865, ABC 16.9, vol. 4.

6. J. F. Clarke, "Journal of Tour Mar. 11-Apr. 11, 1865," Clarke Papers.

7. J. F. Clarke to Dr. Anderson, Nov. 23, 1865, ABC 16.9, vol. 4.

8. Iliev, *Spomeni*, pp. 33, 57, 69.

9. Cited in R. Thomson to Dr. Clark, October 24, 1887, ABC 16.9, vol. 9, part 2.

10. Stanimirov, p. 202.

11. *Missionary News from Bulgaria* 23:6.

12. W. W. Meriam, "Report of the Philippopolis Station for 1860," ABC 16.9, vol. 4.

13. Elias Riggs, "Report of the Constantinople Station of the European Turkey Mission for the year ending April 1, 1898," ABC 16.9, vol. 10; W. W. Sleeper, "Report of the Samokov Station, for the year 1884-5," ABC 16.9, vol. 7.

14. The role of the American Board in the translation of the Bible into modern Bulgarian is studied in detail in Clarke, *Bible Societies*. See, in addition, Elias Riggs, *Reminiscences for My Children*, (unpublished, 1891), pp. 17-26.

15. Elias Riggs, "Report of the Constantinople Station of the European Turkey Mission for the year ending April 11, 1898"; Elias Riggs, "Report of the Constantinople Station of the Eur. T. Mission for the year ending with June 1899," ABC 16.9, vol. 10; Edward Riggs, "Elias Riggs, the Veteran Missionary to Turkey," *The Missionary Review of the World*, n.s., 14 (April, 1901): 270.

16. "The New Hymnal," *Samokov News* 2 (November, 1923): 2.

17. "List of Works Published by the European Turkey Mission," ABC 16.9, vol. 11.

18. See, *Zorni͡tsa* (Istanbul), April 9, 1888, pp. 58-59; July 8, 1889, pp. 106-107.

19. Minutes of the 30th Annual Meeting of the Eu. T. M., ABC 16.9, vol. 15; Geo. D. Marsh to J. L. Barton, January 24, 1903, ABC 16.9, vol. 19.

20. Leo Wiener, "America's Share in the Regeneration of Bulgaria (1840-1859)," *Modern Language Notes* 13:80; Man'o Stoi͡anov, *Bŭlgarska vŭzrozhdenska knizhnina*, vol. 1 (Sofia, 1957), pp. 428-430.

21. J. F. Clarke to Rev. N. G. Clark, September 28, 1867, ABC 16.9, vol. 4.

22. T. L. Byington, "The Fifth Annual Report of the Eski Zagra Station," ABC 16.9, vol. 4; J. F. Clarke, "Annual Report of Philippopolis Station for 1867-8," Clarke Papers.

23. A. S. Tsanoff, "Report of the Bulgarian Evangelical Society for the year 1886/7," ABC 16.9, vol. 7.

24. Fred L. Kingsbury to Dr. Clark, November 6, 1893, ABC 16.9, vol. 13; *Missionary News from Bulgaria* 53:12.

25. Ostrander, p. 35.

26. W. E. Locke, "Records of the 2nd Annual Meeting of the European Turkey Mission," Clarke Papers.

27. J. F. C. 64/1, p. 43, Clarke Papers.

28. R. Thomson to Dr. Barton, August 4, 1897, ABC 16.9, vol. 14; J. F. C. 64/6, p. 379, Clarke Papers.

29. W. P. Clarke, "Annual Report of Samokove Station, presented to the Mission, March 1896," ABC 16.9, vol. 10; Ursula Clarke Marsh to Rev. W. W. Rand, April 30, 1902, Haskell Papers.

30. J. W. Baird, "Annual Report of Monastir Station for the year 1875-6," ABC 16.9, vol. 5.

31. Karavelov, p. 34.

32. See, for example, *Makedonii͡a*, December 13, 1869; January 3, 1870; September 28, 1871.

33. N. Nachov, *T͡sarigrad kato kulturen t͡sentŭr na bŭlgarite do 1877 godina*, (Sofia, 1925), pp. 166-168.

34. Elias Riggs to Dr. Clark, March 15, 1881, ABC 16.9, vol. 9, part 2; Elias Riggs, Robert Thomson to Dr. Clarke /sic/, February 27, 1890, ABC 16.9, vol. 11.

35. R. Thomson to Dr. Clark, April 13, 1886, ABC 16.9, vol. 9, part 2.

36. J. W. Baird to N. G. Clark, July 12, 1894, ABC 16.9, vol. 11.

37. Edward B. Haskell, *American Influence*, pp. 3-4.

38. George D. Marsh, "Report of the Philippopolis Station for year ending April 2, 1912," Haskell Papers.

39. Ian Vagner, "Ot knigata 'Iz evropeiskii͡a Iztok. Ochertsi ot putuvanii͡ata mi iz Bulgarii͡a, Tur͡tsii͡a, Germanii͡a i Rusia," Ianko Bucharov, ed., *Bulgarii͡a prez pogleda na cheshki pŭteshestveni͡tsi* (Sofia, 1984), p. 243.

40. T. L. Byington, "Report of the Constantinople station of the European Turkey Mission for the year 1877-78," Clarke Papers.

41. Haskell, *American Influence*, p. 4.

42. Ĭordan Nikolov, "Vasil Cholakov i protestantskata propaganda prez Vŭzrazhdaneto," *Istoricheski pregled*, no. 4 (1969), p. 91.

43. J. F. Clarke to N. G. Clark (first draft), October 26, 1876, Clarke Papers.

44. *Report of the Central Committee for the Relief of Distress in Bulgaria and c.*, (Constantinople: A. H. Boyajian, 1877), pp. 14-17.

45. Ibid., p. 29.

46. "The following notes of the relief done after five Turkish massacres. . .," May 29, 1911, Clarke Papers.

47. Eugene Schuyler, *Selected Essays*, (New York: Charles Scribner's Sons, 1901), p. 91.

48. "The following notes."

49. Ibid.

50. E. M. S. /Stone/, "Peeps into Sophia Hospitals during the War," *Missionary News from Bulgaria* 6:3-4.

51. J. F. Clarke, *Report of Relief Work for Bulgaria Refugees from Macedonia*, (Samokov, 1904), pp. 1-2.

52. L. Bond, "Report of Monastir Station for the year ending April 6, 1904," ABC 16.9, vol. 16.

53. W. P. Clarke, "Annual Report of Monastir Station, April 17, 1905," ABC 16.9, vol. 16.

54. George D. Marsh, *Report of the Relief Work in the Adrianople Vilayet, 1904-1906*, (Samokov: Mission School Press, n.d.).

55. J. W. Baird, "Report of Samokov Station for the year 1903-1904," ABC 16.9, vol. 16.

56. L. F. Ostrander to J. L. Barton, August 4, 1904, ABC 16.9, vol. 20.

57. Cited in "Pomoganie na stradalt͡si," *Zornit͡sa* (Plovdiv), February 10, 1905, p. 2.

58. Ellen R. Baird, "Report of Woman's Work in Samokove Station for the year 1903-4," ABC 16.9, vol. 16.

59. W. Edwin Locke, "Annual Report of Samokove Station 1880 and 81," ABC 16.9, vol. 7.

60. F. L. Kingsbury to Dr. Clark, November 10, 1882, ABC 16.9, vol. 8.

61. F. L. Kingsbury to Dr. Clark, October 5, 1885, ABC 16.9, vol. 8; F. L. Kingsbury to Dr. Clark, January 7, 1886, ABC 16.9, vol. 8.

62. "Zaveshtanie na Khristodul Kostov Sichanov, May 13, 1889, Samokov," Clarke Papers; Mother to Edward /M. Haskell to E. B. Haskell/, July 16, 1889, Haskell Papers.

63. James F. Clarke, "Report of Samokov Station 1891-2," ABC 16.9, vol. 10; "Report of Medical Work of Samokov Station, 8 April, 1898," ABC 16.9, vol. 10.

64. Fred L. Kingsbury to Dr. Alden, January 6, 1893, ABC 16.9, vol. 13.

65. James F. Clarke to the Members of the European Turkey Mission, July 6, 1899 /Report of Samokov Station for 1898/, ABC 16.9, vol. 10.

66. W. E. Locke, "Annual Report of Philippopolis Station 1889-1890," ABC 16.9, vol. 7.

67. W. E. Locke, "Annual Report of Philippopolis Station 1887 and 8," ABC 16.9, vol. 7.

68. Zoe A. M. Locke, "Temperance in Bulgaria," *Missionary News from Bulgaria* 21:6.

69. J. F. Clarke, "Temperance in Bulgaria," *The Union Signal* (Evanston, Illinois), November 30, 1911, p. 1.

70. J. F. Clarke, "Annual report of Samokov Station, for 1892-3," ABC 16.9, vol. 10.

71. *Missionary News from Bulgaria* 55:1.

72. *Zornit͡sa* (Plovdiv), April 16, 1909, p. 3.

73. Clarke, "Temperance Reform," pp. 1-2.

74. Kh. L-v, "D-r I͡akov Klark," *Trezvo dete* /undated newspaper clipping/, Clarke Papers.

CHAPTER IV
MISSIONARIES AND BULGARIANS: THEIR PERCEPTIONS, ATTITUDES AND UNDERSTANDING OF EACH OTHER

1. *The Missionary Response to the Bulgarians*

A significant portion of the men and women sent to live and work among the Bulgarians by the American Board spent most of their active lives in that country. Even those who were present only for a short period of time were able to form opinions of the natives that were shared in correspondence or in official missionary publications. The American perception of the Bulgarian population was multi-faceted, complex and, at times, contradictory. It touched upon different aspects of Bulgarian society and often revealed not only contemporary developments, but also the missionary mentality.

As soon as they settled in Bulgarian lands, American Board representatives recorded their observations about the character of the Bulgarians they encountered daily. One of the first impressions regarded the similarities between people in the United States and people in Bulgaria. Typically, the missionaries would write about features they found familiar and close to their own background. In March 1860, for example, J. F. Clarke wrote optimistically from Philippopolis:

> In many things the character of the people reminds us of N. England. Their sympathies are strong, their manners courteous, and their minds active, and they seem destined. . .to take a leading place among these nations.(1)

Most likely, this view of the Bulgarian character was influenced by feelings of nostalgia which must have accompanied the great transition that the missionaries underwent in their move to distant lands. In spite of such possibilities, one important element in this statement is the vision of the Bulgarians as people with a promising future, people who by virtue of this became a worthy missionary investment. These were precisely the views of the American Board as voiced by H. G. O. Dwight, one of the first to have hands-on experience of European Turkey. In his words, "the Bulgarians are a rising people, who will repay any amount of missionary labor that may be bestowed upon them."(2)

These early remarks reveal a large amount of hopefulness and assuredness that indeed the task before the missionaries should be a worthy and promising one. As the years progressed, the Americans continued to find the character of the natives as a most valuable potential for their future. For example, J. W. Baird stated in the beginning of 1873 that he detected in many Bulgarians "good material" which had only to be "developed by the Gospel."(3) G. D. Marsh similarly wrote during the same year that the natives "have good natural qualities and only need the right culture of mind and heart to prepare them for great good."(4)

An underlying sense of superiority is clearly detected in these statements. Missionary thinking seems to revolve around two main points—the promising nature of the Bulgarian population as the object of missionary work and the inherent ability of the Americans to perform that task.

The generally good disposition that the Americans displayed toward the Bulgarians was often manifested at times when the latter were not exclusively regarded as potential recipients of the Protestant message. Commenting on the liberation of a large portion of the Bulgarians and their ability to lead an independent existence, certain missionaries saw reasons to praise the people in their newly reestablished state. Thus, T. L. Byington wrote in March, 1880:

> The Bulgarians have done well, very well since the war /the Russo-Turkish War of 1877-1878/. My admiration for them has been steadily increasing... By their own efforts chiefly they had prepared themselves for the great political changes of the past few years.(5)

These lines read as if they were written by a political correspondent rather than a missionary. Perhaps the Americans in European Turkey fulfilled both functions.

Apparently, the representatives of the American Board, by virtue of being the only American presence in the region, felt compelled to act not only as missionaries but also as suppliers of information about a largely unknown people and country. In the case of Byington's pronouncements, the information was certainly sympathetic to the Bulgarians.

In publications designed to spread knowledge of this distant nation to the American public, the missionaries as a rule emphasized the positive impressions acquired in the course of their stay in Bulgaria. J. H. House, for example, in an article that came out in *Missionary Herald* (from October 1882), elaborated on opinions about the Bulgarians. He found them to possess "a strong love of political independence," which to him bore "a strong resemblance to the Anglo-Saxon race." House also stressed that the Bulgarians were "not without courage in war, although they have been a subject race for. . .five hundred years."(6) In addition to containing a very favorable review of the Bulgarian character, House's article again demonstrates the missionary inclination to compare the natives to people of the United States. Generally, comparisons along these lines produced the most positive missionary evaluations of the Bulgarians.

Another missionary, W. W. Sleeper, wrote regarding the Serbian-Bulgarian War of 1885 that: "The Bulgarians are certainly the Americans of So. Eastern Europe." In addition, he characterized them as "long-suffering, ill-treated, betrayed, but liberty-loving people, ready to die in defence of their native land."(7) There is a tendency in comments like Sleeper's and House's for the missionaries to identify themselves with the natives, in particular with native accomplishments and difficulties. The Americans were certainly taking a deep interest in the Bulgarian nation, an interest which was not at all limited to the effort to evangelize them. One of the missionary women wrote in a personal letter, dated November 1887, "I feel great sympathy for this /the Bulgarian/ people in their efforts to rise."(8) Clearly, an attachment to the country and its people was developing in the course of the years in some missionary hearts. For instance, Mary M. Haskell, daughter of H. C. Haskell and a Bulgarian missionary-teacher wrote in 1895 about how much she liked this "*little*, young country... so beautiful by nature /Haskell's emphasis/."(9) Almost in maternal fashion, this American shared her feelings for an adopted child—the Bulgarian nation.

Other Americans in the European Turkey Mission expressed an attitude toward the natives which very closely approximated a relationship with a favorite. In 1907, R. Thomson described his feelings with a great deal of enthusiasm: "It is a delight to live in the midst of a young, progressive nation, with high aspirations, and with a great future (as I believe) before it."(10) The satisfaction of being present in Bulgaria at an important stage of its modern history was coupled with an unqualified approval of what Thomson witnessed.

The missionaries' highly positive evaluation of the Bulgarians' first steps as independent people penetrated the missionary audience and the interested U. S. public to such a degree that in 1912, for example, Theodore Roosevelt himself commented extremely favorably on the subject. In a statement which the missionaries thereafter quoted frequently, he suggested that: "No other nation has travelled so far and so fast as Bulgaria has travelled in the last third of a century."(11)

The positive comments on the abilities of the Bulgarian people sound almost as if the missionaries of the European Turkey Mission had a love-affair with the object of their missionary zeal. Such an impression is not quite correct, however, since in the area of attitudes changes and contradictions are common; moreover, different missionaries differed in their views of the natives. While some could easily be labelled partial to the Bulgarians in proclaiming them "the Americans" of the region, others—actually the majority—had a tendency to report less commendably about the Bulgarians.

Most of the negative remarks about the Bulgarians were related to the realization that Protestant evangelizing could not easily influence them. One missionary, for example, was convinced that the Bulgarians were "careless and worldly."(12) Byington, who wrote admiringly of the natives in 1880, held a negative view of them by 1861. He concluded that centuries of foreign domination had led to "a strong tendency to destroy whatever honesty and manly independence they may have originally possessed." Hence, the Bulgarians could not be trusted and they lacked moral courage.(13) The disappointment among the missionaries in regard to some features of Bulgarian character was so real that at a Convention of Bulgarian Missionaries in 1863 several "unfavorable points of character /which had/ developed among the Bulgarians, such as ingratitude /and/ deceit"(14) were specifically recorded.

The missionaries continuously mentioned Bulgarian shortcomings of a moral nature in combination with the observation that the natives were indisposed to receive the Protestant message. Byington was the author of a gloomy comment illustrating this point. In a letter dated September 1864, he wrote: "The moral atmosphere of Bulgaria is chilling and the obstacles which oppose the introduction of pure Christianity are great."(15)

Missionary correspondence is full of comments reflecting the ruin of the initial hopes for quick and decisive success of the work among a people who at first seemed very willing to reform its religion. The progressing disillusionment among the Americans is frequently recorded in a way which provides an additional insight into the attitude of the foreigners toward the natives. In 1864, Byington concluded that the efforts to preach the Gospel in the preceding five years had shown that the Bulgarians had no wish to hear the missionaries.(16) C. F. Morse, on the other hand, stated in 1865 that the natives like all "Eastern people" were "little accustomed to reasoning."(17)

The list of Bulgarian failures grew longer in the subsequent years. In 1873, J. W. Baird considered the peasants to be "uneducated, superstitious, given to lying."(18) The following year, J. H. House observed that in spite of signs of thought and agitation, "the leaders of the people are almost to a man opposed to the truth," many of the teachers were "infidels," and "drunkenness prevails among the people to an alarming extent."(19) A negative picture of the Bulgarian moral character was drawn whenever it became clear that the missionaries themselves had failed in their original plans to convert the natives. It seems that Bulgarian shortcomings translated into reflection of a general lack of success on the part of the missionaries.

The missionaries continued throughout the 1870s to voice complaints about "ignorance, superstition, and intemperance."(20) Simultaneously, they accused the Bulgarians of duplicity. According to J. W. Baird, they "assent to everything,...talk as piously as they can but in reality...pay no attention to the truth and...do what they openly confess is wrong."(21) Frustrated at their inability to make a decisive impact on religious life in Bulgaria, missionaries like Baird were able to deal with the fact by pointing out that the lack of success was due to native character and behaviour. Typically for speculations of that kind, he did not question the American Board's involvement in European Turkey but reiterated statements about Bulgarian inadequacies.

On occasion, the reflections on the condition of the local people would turn into observations regarding the missionary state of mind in such surroundings. One of the women teachers, for example, wrote about the missionary dependency on "home sympathy" while they were "shut in among these high mud walls."(22) The same sense of frustration and even despair permeates the writings of another American woman, the wife of H. C. Haskell, who felt the need to complain in 1889 that the natives do not realize "the sacrifice we have made in coming here."(23) One should search for explanations for statements like this not only in the direction of the natural feeling of nostalgia exhibited by the missionaries but also in the missionary attitude that the Bulgarians and their way of life were ultimately inferior to the American.

Some of the missionaries stated explicitly that Bulgaria was an uncivilized country. Such was the case of Esther Maltbie, directress of the school for girls in Samokov, whose comments to that effect were published in 1897 in the United States.(24) Others, like G. D. Marsh, were determined to let the natives know of their inability "of deciding unerringly the questions which most of us feel often in doubt about."(25) The latter comment was directed at the native Protestants, but it is still a clear illustration of the tendency among many of the European Turkey Mission to regard the Bulgarians as not entirely equal.

Thus, there were missionaries who seriously doubted that Bulgarians should have their own state following the Russo-Turkish War of 1877-1878. In a letter dated April 1879, W. E. Locke wrote that the Bulgarian population was "no better fitted to govern—to legislate than were the Negroes of the South."(26) Such apprehensions continued to be shown in subsequent years. There was general recognition of the "progress made in ability for self-government"*;(27) however, this was probably not very satisfying to L. Bond who in 1903 preferred to see the Bulgarians of Macedonia "under a strong European government" which would aid them in developing "excellent traits."(28) It appeared logical to this American that if the natives needed outside help in religious affairs, they might also profit from foreign, specifically European, rule. One would hardly expect such statesman-like recommendations from a missionary who might be more occupied with spiritual matters.

Other members of the Mission did not welcome foreign, i.e., non-American, influences in the region. In 1889, H. C. Haskell wrote that the natives "ape the French a good deal." His examples of Bulgarian imitation of the French included the facts that they established a legislative Assembly in the country and that the "roads are divided into kilometers."(29) This missionary did not appreciate such innovations, presumably due to their supposed French origin.

During the several decades of missionary presence in the region, one observation regarding the native people overshadows the rest. The Americans continually noted the Bulgarian concern about political and national matters which they, the missionaries, found harmful and improper. During the first years of the existence of a mission among the Bulgarians, Byington wrote that the natives "are evidently deluding themselves as to the cause of their evils... The Turkish Govt. and the Greek Church are made to bear the whole burden."(30) The leaders of the people were seen as caring for national unity, which in turn prevented them from seriously considering Protestantism.(31) The mass of the Bulgarians were described in 1862 as being "in a state of restless expectancy looking evidently for some important change in their national affairs."(32)

As soon as the missionaries came to know the intense attention which the Bulgarians gave to political and national

* To some contemporary English-speaking authorities on the region, the American missionaries were an important factor in the political maturing of the Bulgarians. The Marquis of Bath wrote, for example, that missionary "teaching has permeated all Bulgarian society, and is not the least important of the causes that have rendered the people capable of wisely using the freedom so suddenly conferred upon them." (See "Extract from 'Observations on Bulgarian Affairs' by the Marquis of Bath," ABC 16.9, vol. 5.).

subjects, they realized that this would be a great obstacle to their work. In 1863, J. F. Clarke wrote in the annual report of the Philippopolis Station that the desire among the native people "to be known as a distinct nation—seems,. . .to fill the vision as to shut out everything Divine,"(33) The problem facing the American Board in European Turkey was carefully presented by L. Bond in a letter dated March 1870:

> The chief barrier now appears to be the ruling idea of nationality. They regard the nation as bound together by their religion, and an acceptance of Protestantism involves separation. How to be both a Bulgarian and a Protestant seems incomprehensible.(34)

The Americans understood that the reason contact with the natives would hardly be productive was twofold—the people did not have time or willingness to contemplate religious questions, and even if there was such inclination, Protestant Christianity would be regarded as divisive and unpatriotic.

During times of particularly great turmoil and change, the Americans continued to complain about their difficulty in approaching the people. The Russo-Turkish War and the Liberation of Bulgaria, for example, received the following comment: "The great political and military events of the year /1878/. . .have occupied the thoughts of the people to such an extent as to render it difficult for us to interest people in religious matters."(35)J. W. Baird made the same observation regarding the Bulgarians who remained under Turkish rule after 1878. Writing from Monastir in 1880, he maintained that the people "are so much in fear of the gov't and so angry at it for its tyranny that it is hard to interest them in any other subject."(36) At such times, the missionaries seemed relatively understanding; the difficulties of war and foreign oppression could not be put aside.

There was one occasion, however, when the missionaries could not bring themselves to be understanding toward Bulgarian political and national goals. They unanimously condemned the kidnapping of Ellen Stone in the early 1900s by local revolutionaries attempting to extract money. Protestant Bulgarians who also placed national concerns before religious duties were the greatest disappointment. J. F. Clarke found it difficult to comprehend that the pastor of the Bansko church "was doubtless a leader in insurrectionary movements."(37) J. W. Baird was indignant that missionaries were told to their "faces by leading Protestants that events have justified Miss Stone's captivity."(38) The disillusionment with the native followers was even greater following the unsuccessful rebellion in the region of Macedonia in 1903. Baird concluded from Samokov that many Bulgarian Protestants were persuaded that "the freeing of Macedonia is at present of greater importance than the spread of the Gospel among their countrymen."(39)

The trying years of insurrections, wars, and general political unrest certainly did not contribute to the normal functioning of the mission. The missionaries recognized this fact and repeatedly voiced their concern about the impact of the times not only upon mission work but also upon the people. Just prior to the beginning of the Balkan Wars, one American spoke of the "scars of the revolutionary movement on the character of many," referring to the inhabitants of Macedonia.(40) Others considered the Bulgarians "a people that look haughtily at anything religious that is not connected with the Eastern Church."(41)

Thus, the period of National Revival in the Bulgarian lands was presented in missionary writing to show that while making the activities of the American Board at all possible in the region, the spirit of the times also severely limited the purely religious aspects of these activities. Whether complaining, understanding, or rejecting the workings of the nationalist ideas among the natives, the missionaries were clear in pointing out that Bulgarian concern for political independence and unity was the major stumbling block in the way of spreading Protestantism.

There were, naturally, variations in the manner in which the local people reacted to the missionary presence. During the second half of the nineteenth century, the Americans frequently reported signs of encouragement in terms of the Bulgarian attitude. One of the first statements to this effect came from J. F. Clarke who was glad to see in 1867 that "educated men value and gladly avail themselves of the results of missionary labor."(42) He was commenting on the favorable native response given to textbooks translated in the Mission. The following year, Clarke asserted that "thinking persons" in the country "are favorably disposed towards and have a degree of confidence in us."(43) Such indications of limited Bulgarian acceptance of the missionaries became more pronounced during and after the April Uprising of 1876. In May 1876, for example, still the early phase of the uprising, L. Bond informed Boston that "the leaders of the rebellion. . .openly assert that Protestants are as good patriots as any."(44) The missionary considered this an indication that Bulgarians no longer regard their church as all important to the question of national independence. Several months later, Bond observed that "the natives have been much more friendly toward us ever since the troubles /the uprising and its defeat/ began."(45) There was no illusion about the new friendliness exhibited by the Bulgarians during this critical time. Nevertheless, the Americans were willing to interpret this as "doors wide open" for their work.(46)

Reports of such "hopeful" signs appeared in 1879 and 1880 when G. D. Marsh observed that the Bulgarians seemed ready to accept influence and that they appreciated American, but not necessarily Protestant, institutions.(47) During the 1880s and 1890s, there were only a few missionary comments regarding wider possibilities for preaching and spiritual awakening in Bulgaria.(48) For the twentieth century, no similar reports exist, a fact which indicated that the natives did not come to look more favorably on the European Turkey Mission.

The Americans' view of the Bulgarians varied greatly from missionary to missionary and from time to time. There are several features in the complexity of missionary opinions, however, which seem in part to fit a model, developed by a linguist-turned-historian, Tzvetan Todorov, in a study of the highly successful effort on the part of Westerners to influence and assimilate the American Indians.(49) Much like the behavior of the European conquerors, the representatives of the American Board in Bulgaria had the "capacity to understand the other." This ability was accompanied by a feeling of superiority on the part of the Americans which, according to Todorov, is the important second element of the model of assimilation. The writings by the missionaries reveal also the third required component— "temporary identification with the other," in this case, the other being the Bulgarian population. Todorov's model concludes with a fourth element: reassertion of Western identity and assimilation of the Indians. While the American missionaries preserved their identity in writing and/or actions, they were certainly not able to assimilate the native population. In fact, complete assimilation was never their goal, which indicated the one important difference in the case of the American missionary presence in Bulgaria; the object of American pressures (i.e., the native population) was not sufficiently different from the foreigners. Both the Americans and the Bulgarians were Christian, and both, in part, shared a similar European heritage.

In spite of these important distinctions, Todorov's model is largely applicable to the European Turkey Mission's attempt to convert an entire nation. While this model may serve to illustrate certain universal features of missionary thinking and behavior in Bulgaria, it also brings out points of difference which in turn offer a plausible explanation for the general lack of large-scale success in the European Turkey Mission. It is useful, therefore, to pursue at greater length the question of the natives and their response to the American presence in the region.

2. *The Bulgarian Response to the Missionaries*

> In the popular mind a protestant is "one who does not drink intoxicating liquors, does not smoke, does not keep the fasts, and goes every Sunday to church with two books under his arm."*

The Bulgarians responded to the settlement of the first American missionaries with apprehension and bewilderment. Some regarded them as "uninvited guests"(50) while others had more definite ideas about the newcomers, but as a rule, the most common reaction was one of opposition. According to one native of Philippopolis, the Protestant missionaries had come in order "to spoil Orthodoxy and to remove the Bulgarians from Russian tutelage."(51) Suspected of such

* A. D. Gulumanoff, "Bulgaria and the Bulgarian Protestants," (read assembly hour, Oberlin, May 8, 1912), Haskell Papers.

ominous plans, the Americans were subjected to a great deal of unfriendliness during their entire stay in the country. As H. C. Haskell remembered, twenty-five years after his arrival in Bulgarian lands, they were viewed "with all the suspicion and opposition with which a company of Jesuit missionaries working among the families attending Protestant churches in Boston, Cleveland or Chicago would be regarded!" (52)

The strangeness and the lack of knowledge about the foreigners were certainly factors contributing to the first impressions they made on the natives. Their attempts to communicate using the Bulgarian language were difficult to comprehend. A man residing in present-day Pazardzhik remembered that he and his neighbors reacted with amazement to the missionaries' "useless" attempts to talk to the local people in Bulgarian.(53) At other locations, the people did not want to have anything to do with the Americans and demonstrated their attitude very clearly. For example, C. F. Morse, when referring to his welcome in Sofia during 1862-1863, "considered it a special favor of Providence that we /the missionaries/ have been permitted to live among them /the Bulgarians/ unmolested."(54)

The Bulgarian feelings of suspicion gradually evolved into direct dislike as the newcomers revealed more and more about their way of life and reasoning. Morse reported in 1864, again from Sofia, that all local people had turned against him and his co-workers as soon as it became clear that they did not observe fasts and did not cross themselves.(55) In Philippopolis, the residents were scandalized following the incident of an Orthodox monk who was given missionary protection when he promised to convert if allowed to marry. The event took place in 1865 and it reconfirmed suspicions among the Bulgarians that nothing good could be expected from the strangers. The Russian Consul in the city, Naiden Gerov, described the feelings of the native people, both Christian and Moslem, in a report to his superior in Istanbul. According to Gerov, the local population "considers the Protestants to be godless men, who do not hold anything as sacred and who allow themselves anything."(56)

The treatment reserved for the missionaries everywhere in the country was not only unkindly but occasionally violent. In towns like Sopot, for example, the local priest warned the people against the Protestants who had "come as foxes to catch them."(57) As a result no one came near the missionaries. At other locations, the Americans were not so fortunate as to be left alone. Panagiurishte became the scene of ugly insults and the throwing of stones.(58)

By the second half of the 1860s, the Americans reported that the general atmosphere which surrounded them was one of hostility and indifference. They were anathematized by Orthodox priests, assaulted by mobs of people, and in general, treated like unwelcome intruders.(59)

In fact, during the entire period considered in this study, the missionaries again and again experienced severe persecution. Among the more drastic cases, only a few will be mentioned here to illustrate the difficulties which the members of the American Board experienced as they tried to fit into Bulgarian society. During the early 1870s, a missionary woman together with a native helper were attacked at a guest house in the village of Merichleri. As a result, a wall of the building was damaged. In Panagiurishte in 1873, the house of the missionary bookseller was treated in a similar manner. The same year brought even more destruction in Merichleri where the Protestant building serving as a church and a school was entirely demolished.(60) Working in the Principality with its constitutional guarantee of religious freedom did not change missionary fortune substantially. Samokov, one of the centers of the European Turkey Mission, witnessed repeated stoning of missionaries and their families on the streets in the early 1890s. In 1901, in the same city, an attempt was made to set fire to the school for girls. Finally, a Protestant church in the village of Abdulare was burnt in 1910.(61)

Missionary documentation, in addition, was full of records of annoyances of a lesser magnitude. Among these were efforts of the Bulgarian Exarchate to ban missionary literature as well as demonstrations in front of the Samokov schools by native students shouting "Down with Protestants, down with Americans."(62)

Clearly, the missionaries were frequently and continuously reminded that at least a portion of the native population was ready to dispel them from Bulgaria. The few converts that they were able to attract were, as a rule, ostracized by relatives, friends, and society, a situation which further illustrates that most Bulgarians rejected Protestantism. In fact, the typical attitude toward native converts was much more harsh than that shown to the Americans. Native Protestants, for example, were abandoned by their families, publicly beaten, forcibly removed from American schools or churches, cursed, and stoned; their businesses were boycotted, and their dead were at times not allowed to be buried anywhere near an Orthodox cemetery.(63) In a Protestant eulogy for a member of one of the first Bulgarian families of converts, it was revealed that:

> the bakers refused to bake their bread in the public ovens, the herders refused to take their goats out to the common pasture; their friends and even their relatives refused to have anything to do with them.(64)

Those natives who were willing to accept the American invitation certainly found it extremely difficult to become and remain Protestant.

The record of Bulgarian unwillingness to allow the missionaries to proceed with their work was surely a long and clear one. Both leaders and ordinary people explained that their resolute actions against Protestantism were necessitated by what they perceived to be the anti-national and divisive nature of that religion. In fact, there was a general consensus among Bulgarians of different political persuasions that the Americans were ultimately bringing harm to the people by dividing them and weakening their struggle against their oppressors. Conservative groups were in full agreement with revolutionaries that Protestantism should not be allowed to spread in Bulgaria due to its inherent divisive nature. In 1866, the Istanbul-based conservative newspaper, *Tur͡tsiia,* expressed the view that the Americans and their native helpers worked "to create parties among the people."(65) Politicians such as G. S. Rakovski and L. Karavelov who were on the opposite end of the Bulgarian ideological spectrum held the same opinion. Rakovski considered the religious unity of his people to be of greatest importance, and he even suggested the creation of a new religious teaching exclusively for Bulgarian use in order to "parry all blows, Catholic, Protestant, Greek and Slavic."(66) Karavelov specifically accused the Protestant missionaries of sowing schisms and disagreements among the Bulgarian people and concluded that: "Our Orthodoxy is related to our freedom and to our Bulgarian nationality...that is why every honest Bulgarian must remain faithful to his own religion."(67) Other leading men among the natives were so concerned about the Protestant "danger" that they published books specifically written in order to discredit the missionaries and their teachings. Examples of such works are two books written by Vasil Cholakov and published in 1870, one publication by Matei Preobrazhenski of the same year,(68) and the above mentioned work by T. Ikonomov. All these authors considered the Americans and their faith to be anti-Bulgarian and divisive. Even Bulgarians, such as P. R. Slaveikov, who cooperated with the European Turkey Mission's non-proselytizing work made clear their complete rejection of Protestant religion as harmful to Bulgarian national unity and the struggle for independence.*

Native anxieties regarding the possible divisive effects of the spread of a new brand of Christianity cannot readily be dismissed as unrealistic or paranoid. The Turks in the region had similar expectations and were glad to welcome the Americans for that reason. W. P. Page mentioned in his correspondence of 1874 that: "The Turks are glad of everything that will help divide the Bulgarians—and they think Protestantism will do it."(69) In 1877, J. F. Clarke encountered the same attitude at a meeting with a Turkish military commander who said, "We are glad to have you *divide* /Clarke's emphasis/ the Bulgarians."(70)

The Bulgarian awareness of Protestantism as a divisive force in national life was the main reason given for its rejection. At times, people combined this opinion with a feeling that the Americans had no place in a land "of churches and schools."(71) Native self-esteem was hurt by the suggestion that the Bulgarians were in need of religious reform and enlightenment. Mikhail Madzharov, who received his education at an American institution, Robert College, and who had even worked for a time for *Zornitsa*, expressed this idea in his memoirs: "Sometimes it seemed insulting to us that foreign missionaries in a bad Bulgarian language criticized the faith of our fathers and forefathers and wanted to show us that they were enlightened and we were savages."(72) In addition, the long and uninterrupted Orthodox tradition was considered far

* Slaveikov's opinion is noted on page 47.

superior to the relative newcomer—Protestantism. The typical reaction was to say: "We have been Christians for over a thousand years, while protestantism is a heretical teaching from the 16th century."(73) It is clear that from a Bulgarian point of view the Americans were carriers of an inferior kind of religion. To a people who withstood five centuries of foreign domination largely due to its separate religious identity, tradition was more important than questions of change.

The Americans certainly touched sensitive areas in the Bulgarian psyché. They offended the native feeling of self-esteem and were generally considered as detrimental to the national unity of the country. The latter accusation was often interpreted to mean that the American Board pursued "double" goals. The Bulgarians believed that the missionaries had certain political aims in Bulgaria, which by virtue of their anti-Orthodox nature, were understood to be anti-Slavic and anti-Russian, in particular. Curiously, contemporary comments to that effect were not numerous or specific. In addition to a previously quoted remark by a resident of Philippopolis (see page 118) and the works by Cholakov and Matei Preobrazhenski noted above, only sporadic newspaper accusations illustrate this attitude.(74)

The Bulgarian perception of the Americans as political agents is particularly emphasized in Bulgarian historiography, which with a few exceptions labels the activity of the European Turkey Mission as investment of American political influence in the region.(75) Some scholars even maintain that the missionaries were aware that their work had "a deep political meaning."(76) All such statements, by contemporaries or by subsequent historians, have never been proven and are difficult to substantiate from all available documentary sources. The missionaries usually had difficulties securing routine government protection for themselves and their work. Their correspondence contains evidence that leading circles in the United States were rarely willing to accommodate missionary needs. Whenever the American Board required official action, it had real problems securing it. Such were the cases of the periodic occurrences of Turkish government harassment or the case of the murder of one missionary by brigands in the early 1860s.(77) The American government considered the Americans in Bulgaria to be so insignificant that no diplomatic representation existed during the entire period covered by this study. In 1882, F. L. Kingsbury expressed the general concern held by himself and his colleagues about this official attitude toward the missionaries; in a letter to Boston, he explained, "Oh, how good it would be to have an American Consul here within the principality but I suppose the Gov't would be unwilling to send any one out to protect us."(78) It appears that the missionaries felt neglected and were not at all promoters of American political interests.

There were only a few incidents when individual missionaries became involved in political matters, but these were related to the promotion of Bulgarian causes. Events surrounding the revolt in Macedonia in 1903 prompted J. F. Clarke and E. B. Haskell to express their energetic support for the Bulgarian population. Clarke prepared an article in which he wrote that "the United States should now *at once* use all the influence possible to secure to Macedonia *at least* autonomous government /Clarke's emphasis/.(79) Haskell's criticism of Turkish rule went so far that he was unofficially scolded by the American Board.(80)

In general, the missionaries stood aloof from political affairs and resisted attempts by native followers to enlist them in nationalist struggles. During the second half of the 1880s, for example, Bulgarian Protestants were pressuring the Americans to take a clear anti-Greek stand in certain areas of Macedonia. The policy of the European Turkish Mission, however, remained neutral and the "native brethren" were advised "to learn to be cautious about making balls for us to throw."(81)

The Bulgarian Protestants again were the ones who advertized everything American to the Bulgarian public and attempted to promote close ties (including political) with the United States. Vatralski, mentioned earlier as highly appreciative of missionary accomplishments in his country, wrote about his desire that Bulgarians should "Americanize their souls" out of gratitude and patriotic considerations.(82) Another Protestant, S. V. T͡sanov, advocated on the pages of *Zorni͡tsa* the establishment of friendly relations with the United States which should further Bulgarian interests in international diplomacy.(83) In contrast, the missionaries were never so outspoken in the treatment of their homeland.

Granted, their followers were dedicated to becoming such ardent Americanophiles, but the Americans themselves were much more moderate in pointing out American attractiveness. While Vatralski wrote about Americanization, his mentors published articles about the advantages of the American political system.(84) This is a typical example of the missionary presentation of issues so closely related to their upbringing. Naturally, they thought and behaved as Americans, but this did not transform into a conscious effort to promote American interests in Bulgaria.

Finally, it is important to emphasize that the United States had negligible involvement in the region, which makes the widespread claim of missionary political intentions even more improbable. In fact, students of American involvement in the Near East consider the missionaries as a major manifestation of American private interest in the region while the navy represented the official interest.(85) Clearly, it is difficult to present the European Turkey Mission as an outpost of American political engagement. It was never regarded as anything other than a private enterprise, and the missionaries sometimes even had difficulty securing regular consular protection as private citizens.

So far, the Bulgarian image of the Protestant missionaries appears to be comprised of negative attitudes. While these views did not always have a sound foundation, they nevertheless comprised the majority perception of the Americans. However, certain Bulgarians held a different view of the missionaries. Some, like P. R. Slaveikov, who rejected Protestantism as a religion for the Bulgarian people, were equally opposed to the outbursts of violence against the Americans. On the pages of Slaveikov's *Makedonii͡a*, readers found rebukes to such "Medieval" approaches to the foreigners.(86) Others willingly accepted knowledge and help from the missionaries. A native of Eski Zagra wrote about his appreciation of Protestant literature. A man from Samokov explained his toleration of the newcomers in the following remark: "Shall I refuse bread when hungry and eat stones because a Protestant offers me bread?"(87) Similar more practical acceptance of the missionaries was demonstrated in the late 1870s when the members of the European Turkey Mission reported a favorable change in native reception.

Examples of native appreciation of some aspect of the American presence continued to be sporadically felt in the subsequent years. A good example of kinder treatment is what occurred in the town of Resen where the missionaries were instrumental in ending a longstanding quarrel between two influential Orthodox families. At a neighboring place, the Bulgarians presented the Americans a generous dinner in their honor.(88)

There are few additional examples of better treatment provided by the mass of Orthodox people, and even the few that are mentioned above are not related to the proselytizing nature of the missionary involvement. Clearly, the native perception of the American Board and its representatives tended to be rather negative, often bordering on total rejection. It did not reveal any important contradictions or changes among different groups of people during different periods of time. Even on the relatively rare occasions when the Bulgarians considered the missionaries acceptable, they were not commenting on the religious capacity of the Americans. In addition to the limited acceptance of Protestant educational and literary work discussed above, these instances of toleration demonstrate a more practical attitude toward the effects of mission presence. In the words of S. Stambulov, a leading Bulgarian statesman, who spoke as Prime Minister in 1892, his sympathy with the American missionaries was due to his impression of them as "invaluable promoters of civilization."(89) No Bulgarian, except the small number of converts, ever recorded his appreciation of their religious plans. Evidently, the strictly Protestant aspect of missionary work in Bulgaria was rejected by the majority of the natives, while a limited minority accepted certain other aspects of American involvement.

List of References

1. J. F. Clarke to Dr. Anderson, March 7, 1860, ABC 16.9, vol. 4.

2. Cited in Charles F. Morse to N. G. Clark, June 8, 1867, ABC 16.9, vol. 4.

3. J. W. Baird to Sec. Clark, February 15, 1873, ABC 16.9, vol. 5.

4. G. D. Marsh to Sec. Clark, March 10, 1873, ABC 16.9, vol. 6.

5. T. L. Byington to Dr. Clark, March 20, 1880, ABC 16.9, vol. 5.

6. J. H. House, "Village Life in Bulgaria," /reprinted from *Missionary Herald*, October, 1882/, *The Bulgarians* (n.p., n.d.), pp. 9, 12.

7. W. W. Sleeper to N. G. Clark, November 19, 1885, ABC 16.9, vol. 9, part 2.

8. Mother /M. H. Haskell/ to E. B. Haskell, November 21, 1887, Haskell Papers.

9. Mary M. Haskell to James L. Barton, March 23, 1895, ABC 16.9, vol. 12.

10. R. Thomson, "Missionary Life and Work in Bulgaria, as I see it," ABC 16.9, vol. 20.

11. Cited in /P. Rowland/, *The Samokov American Schools. Sixty Years of Service in Bulgaria*, (Boston, 1924), p. 5.

12. W. F. Arms to Dr. Anderson, July 16, 1860, ABC 16.9, vol. 4.

13. T. L. Byington, "The Second Annual Report of the Eski Zagra Station," ABC 16.9, vol. 4.

14. A. L. Long, "Convention of Bulgarian Missionaries. Eski Zagra May 6, 1883," Clarke Papers.

15. T. L. Byington to Dr. Anderson, September 13, 1864, ABC 16.9, vol. 4.

16. T. L. Byington to Dr. Anderson, October 11, 1864, ABC 16.9, vol. 4.

17. Charles F. Morse, "Third Report of the Sophia Station," ABC 16.9, vol. 4.

18. J. W. Baird to Sec. Clark, February 15, 1873, ABC 16.9, vol. 5.

19. J. Henry House, "Report of the Eski Zagra Station for the year ending June 18th, 1874," Clarke Papers.

20. J. Henry House to Dr. Clark, May 30, 1874, ABC 16.9, vol. 8.

21. J. W. Baird, "Annual Report of Monastir Station for the year 1875-6," ABC 16.9, vol. 5.

22. Sophia Crawford to N. G. Clark, May, 1882, ABC 16.9, vol.8.

23. Mother to Edward /M. H. Haskell to E. B. Haskell/, July 16, 1889, Haskell Papers.

24. "Pictures from Samokov," *Life and Light*, (June, 1897), p. 284.

25. G. D. Marsh to J. L. Barton, May 15, 1900, ABC 16.9, vol. 19.

26. W. E. Locke to N. G. Clarke /sic/, April 3, 1879, ABC 16.9, vol. 6.

27. *Missionary News from Bulgaria* 51:7.

28. L. Bond to J. L. Byington, August 18, 1903, ABC 16.9, vol. 17.

29. Father /H. C. Haskell/ to E. B. Haskell, January 25, 1889, Haskell Papers.

30. T. L. Byington, "The First Annual Report of the Eski Zagra Station," Clarke Papers.

31. J. F. Clarke to Dr. Anderson, June 21, 1861, ABC 16.9, vol. 4.

32. Oliver Crane, "Report of the Adrianople Station for the year ending June 1st, 1862," ABC 16.9, vol. 4.

33. J. F. Clarke, "Annual Report of Philippopolis Station for the 1862," Clarke Papers.

34. L. Bond to Gen. Prud. Com. A.B.C.F.M., March 12, 1870, ABC 16.9, vol. 4.

35. J. W. Baird, "Report of Monastir Station for the year ending June 30th 1878," Clarke Papers.

36. J. W. Baird to Sec. Clark, November 30th, 1880, ABC 16.9, vol. 7.

37. J. F. Clarke to J. L. Barton, March 4, 1902, ABC 16.9, vol. 17.

38. J. W. Barid to Dr. Barton, July 6, 1903, ABC 16.9, vol. 17.

39. J. W. Baird to J. L. Barton, October 25, 1905, ABC 16.9, vol. 17.

40. "Report of Salonica Station, Apr. 29, 1910 to Apr. 19, 1911," Clarke Papers.

41. J. B. Baird to Dr. Barton, December 11, 1909, ABC 16.9, vol. 17.

42. J. F. Clarke to Rev. N. G. Clark, September 28, 1867, ABC 16.9, vol. 4.

43. J. F. Clarke to Rev. N. G. Clark, August 31, ABC 16.9, vol. 4.

44. L. Bond to Dr. N. G. Clark, May 12, 1876, ABC 16.9, vol. 5.

45. L. Bond to Dr. N. G. Clark, September 15, 1876, ABC 16.9, vol. 5.

46. W. Edwin Locke, "Annual Report of Samokove Station 1876 and 7," Clarke Papers.

47. G. D. Marsh to N. G. Clark, December 4, 1879, ABC 16.9, vol. 6; G. D. Marsh to N. G. Clark, April 21, 1880, ABC 16.9, vol. 6.

48. E. M. Stone to N. G. Clark, November 22, 1888, ABC 16.9, vol. 9, part 2; Edward B. Haskell, "Report of Salonica Station from April 22, 1897 to April 12, 1898," Clarke Papers.

49. Tzvetan Todorov, *The Conquest of America*, tran. by Richard Howard, (New York: Harper and Row, Publishers, 1984).

50. Dinekov, p. 154.

51. Enicherev, p. 53.

52. H. C. Haskell to N. G. Clark, March 5, 1888, ABC 16.9, vol. 8.

53. *Missionary News from Bulgaria* 18:8.

54. C. F. Morse, "The First Annual Report of the Sophia Station, 1863," ABC 16.9, vol. 4.

55. C. F. Morse, "Report of the Sophia Station being the 2nd Report," ABC 16.9, vol. 4.

56. *Dokumenti za bŭlgarskata istoriia͡*, vol. 1, (Sophia, 1931, p. 404.

57. Henry C. Haskell, "Journal of a Tour North and NorthWest of Philippopolis: March and April 1865," Clarke Papers.

58. James F. Clarke, "Annual Report of Philippopolis Station for 1867-8," Clarke Papers.

59. For examples of such attitude, see, J. F. Clarke to Dr. Clark, September 12, 1866, ABC 16.9, vol. 4; Charles F. Morse, "Report of the Sophia Station for 1867," ABC 16.9, vol. 4; W. Edwin Locke, "Annual Report of the Samokove Station for 1868-9." ABC 16.9, vol. 4.

60. L. Bond, "Report of the Eski Zagra Station for the year ending June 24th, 1872," Clarke Papers; H. P. Page, "Report of Samokove Station for 1872-1873," ABC 16.9, vol. 5; J. Henry House, "Report of the Eski Zaghra Station for the year ending June 18th, 1874," Clarke Papers.

61. F. L. Kingsbury to Dr. Clark, December 24, 1891, ABC 16.9, vol. 13; G. D. Marsh to J. L. Barton, February 19, 1901, ABC 16.9, vol. 19; H. C. Haskell, "Report of the Philippopolis Station of the European Turkey Mission for the Missive Year 1910," Haskell Papers.

62. N. T. Boyadziev, "Report to the Annual Meeting of the European Turkey Mission of the A.B.C.F.M.," ABC 16.9, vol. 10; H. C. Haskell to N. G. Clark, July 12, 1894, ABC 16.9, vol. 12.

63. See examples of such treatment in C. F. Morse, "Report of the Eski Zagra Station for 1867 and 8," ABC 16.9, vol. 4; Henry C. Haskell, "11th Annual Report of the Philippopolis Station, 1869-70," Clarke Papers; Stefan Kazanli͡aklii͡a to K. F. Mors, February 27, 1870, Clarke Papers; L. Bond, "Report of the Eski Zagra Station for the year ending July, 1871," Clarke Papers; Afina to Mrs. Jenney, March 28, 1880, Clarke Papers; J. W. Baird, "Report of Monastir Station, Aug. 10, 1895-March 20, 1896," Clarke Papers; L. Bond, "Report of Monastir Station for the year ending July 3, 1899," Clarke Papers.

64. "Miss Rada Pavlova," *Samokov News* 3 (March, 1925):7.

65. *Turt͡sii͡a* (Istanbul), October 8, 1866.

66. M. Arnaudov, ed., *Arkhiv na G. S. Rakovski*, vol. 1, (Sophia, 1952), p. 249.

67. Karavelov, p. 119.

68. For details about the two authors and their anti-Protestant activities, see, Nikolov, "Vasil Cholakov," pp. 89-102; Iordan Nikolov, "Borbata na Matei Preobrazhenski protiv protestantskata propaganda," *Izvestii͡a na Instituta za istorii͡a* 18:213-230; Atanas Sugarev, "Roli͡ata na chitalishte 'Videlina' v obshtestvenii͡a i kulturen zhivot na Panagi͡urishte," *Panagiurishte i Panagi͡ursko v minaloto*, (Sofia, 1956), pp. 269-286.

69. H. P. Page to Clark, April 11, 1874, ABC 16.9, vol. 6.

70. "The following notes."

71. L. Bond to Drs. E. E. Strong and C. H. Daniels, November 30, 1898, ABC 16.9, vol. 11.

72. Mikhail Madzarov, *Spomeni*, (Sofia, 1968), p. 258.

73. Gulumanoff.

74. Examples cited in Mother /M. H. Haskell/ to Edward B. Haskell, May 24, 1899, Haskell Papers.

75. See, for example, Stoi͡anov, "Nachalo," p. 65 and Shopov, p. 183.

76. Pantev, p. 45.

77. R. Anderson to Hon Wm. H. Seward, August 21, 1862, Clarke Papers; James L. Barton to Edward B. Haskell, April 30, 1908, Haskell Papers.

78. F. L. Kingsbury to Dr. Clark, November 4, 1882, ABC 16.9, vol. 8.

79. J. F. Clarke, "Macedonia and the Capture of Miss Stone," ABC 16.9, vol. 20.

80. E. B. Haskell to Dr. Barton, February 4, 1904, ABC 16.9, vol. 18.

81. L. Bond, "Report of Monastir for the year ending Apr. 16, 1889," Clarke Papers. More on this subject may be found in W. E. Locke to N. G. Clark, September 23, 1885, ABC 16.9, vol. 9, part 1.

82. Vatralski, p. 362.

83. *Zorni͡tsa* (Plovdiv), January 20, 1905, p. 4.

84. See a series of unsigned articles, "Bulgarii͡a i Sŭedinenite Dŭrzhavi u Amerika," *Zorni͡tsa* (Istanbul), January 4, 1879, p. 2; January 11, 1879, p. 6; January 18, 1889, p. 10; February 1, 1879, p. 18.

85. James A. Field, Jr., "Trade, Skills, and Sympathy: The First Century and a Half of Commerce with the Near East," *The Annals of the American Academy of Political and Social Science*, 401:9.

86. *Makedonii͡a*, April 20, 1871.

87. Cited in "Notes of Tour of Rev. Wm. W. Meriam, Frid. April 4 to Sat. May 10, 1862," Clarke Papers. See also, Iliev, pp. 33, 57.

88. L. Bond, "Report of Monastir Station for the three months ending Dec. 31, 1899," ABC 16.9, vol. 10.

89. Cited in Sir Edwin Pears, *Forty Years in Constantinople*, (New York: D. Appleton and Company, 1916), p. 194.

CONCLUSION

> So long as Western civilization was essentially Catholic or Protestant, it was unacceptable to Orthodox peoples. When it became primarily scientific and secular, it was acceptable, and even desirable...*

For more than half a century, the American Board continuously involved itself in the task of converting the Bulgarian nation to Protestantism. In pursuit of this goal, the missionaries settled among a population largely unknown to them and energetically began their work. As they gathered more and more first hand information about the Bulgarians, the Americans extended their activities in different, but not strictly religious, areas. They were thus engaged in Bulgarian education and literary life, in addition to the day-to-day task of evangelizing the natives. Certain of these activities were initiated due to Bulgarian demands or needs (e.g., education, publishing and other literary efforts, philanthropy). The rest, together with the work of conversion, were largely unsolicited and unwanted by the local population. Not surprisingly, the outcome of various missionary endeavors proved to depend extensively on Bulgarian reception. Certainly, the great success of the Protestant newspapers could hardly be compared to the numerically negligible results of native evangelization. Similar to this most striking example, the Bulgarians tended to allow the missionary presence to be felt in welcome spheres of activity but rejected it in those considered undesirable. Missionary perseverance was mostly responsible for the establishment of any foothold in the sphere of conversion to Protestantism.

Parallel to the effectiveness of the different American engagements was the native comprehension of both

* L. S. Stavrianos, "The Influence of the West on the Balkans," Charles and Barbara Jelavich, eds., *The Balkans in Transition. Essays on the Development of Balkan Life and Politics Since the Eighteenth Century.* (Archon Books, 1974), p. 188.

missionaries and their aims. As a rule, kind treatment was reserved for the foreigners in their non-Protestant capacity while frequently violent rejection was manifested toward the effort to gain converts. Therefore, the members of the European Turkey Mission were functioning in a contradictory atmosphere of encouragement and discouragement which, however, did not interfere with their rather persistent view of their final goals and tasks in Bulgaria.

The attempt to gain an understanding of the missionary and native perceptions of different aspects of the American presence in the country, established that while the final Protestant aim remained the same, changes occurred in the way the representatives of the New World evaluated the effect of their work. Often, the initial purpose was completely abandoned in favor of new criteria. The Americans' educational involvement is a case in point. Originally viewed as a vehicle to gain access to the natives, the enterprise was later evaluated in terms of its general effect on the entire population. The same element of change took place in the literary and even proselytizing efforts. This change actually reflected the unintended results of most missionary initiatives. Native attitude determined these results and not missionary planning. In the words of James L. Barton, a secretary of the American Board "The Bulgarians...welcomed the missionaries with their new literature and education as calculated to strengthen them as a nation."(1)

The peculiarities of the Bulgarian National Revival, which emphasized nationalist ideas, at the same time determined the outcome of the American plans for Bulgaria. While cultural activities were generally appreciated as an aid in the emancipation of the people, the Bulgarians rejected the Protestant message because they felt it undermined the unifying influence of Orthodoxy on the nation. This places the native population in a position differing from that of a passive receiver of the conscious missionary attempt for religious change and, instead, places it in the position of a selective participant in two-way interaction. The case of the European Turkey Mission might serve to illustrate similar substance in a larger development—Western impact on the Balkan region, in general.

Another important component in the American presence among the Bulgarians was the complex and often contradictory perception of the natives in the missionary mind. Oscillating between two extremes—one of infatuation and one of rejection of certain basic features of what the missionaries considered the Bulgarian character and way of life, this image was made known to interested groups of the American public in the form of various publications and missionary correspondence. In this way, the Protestants in Bulgaria served as disseminators of information in the United States about a small and distant nation. By virtue of being the only American presence in the region, they also became "America's most important source of information about" that part of the world.(2)

The reverse of this process was the propagation in Bulgarian lands of knowledge about both the United States and the American way of life. Generally demonstrating a feeling of superiority, but honestly intended, the missionaries became instrumental in the flow of Western ideas throughout the Balkan Peninsula. Opening new "windows" to the native awareness of the outside world, the Americans again acted as disseminators of information—this time for the local people.

Clearly, the missionaries of the American Board in European Turkey were filling "many shoes" simultaneously in the course of going about their first and foremost task—the promotion of Protestantism. This small group of people acted as missionaries, teachers, journalists, publishers, philanthropists, promoters of temperance ideas, translators, and even writers. The variety of their roles is quite impressive; at the same time, it indicates a probably unwise utilization of energies. It will never be known whether by concentrating on just a few areas the missionaries might have been more successful. The extent of their various involvements in native life, however, is a credit to their creativity and ability. It also might be interpreted as evidence of flexibility in the ongoing search for the best way to find access to Bulgarian minds and souls.

The statistical evaluation of the American Board's work in Bulgaria further illustrates the somewhat frenzied state of the missionary effort. The reaching of so many different villages, towns and cities, the attracting of so many natives in the various American educational institutions, the printing of an enormous amount of missionary and other literature, all indicate, among many other things, that much was done in the European Turkey Mission. However, it is more important to ask, as did one of the native helpers* — how much was accomplished by both American and Bulgarian standards.

From the missionary point of view, the original and, at the same time, final goal was definitely out of reach, at least for the foreseeable future. Virtually in all spheres of activity, their accomplishments fell short of their original purpose. If the foreigners could claim to have affected some meaningful impact, it was the fact that they aided the emancipation of a people who had survived for five centuries under Ottoman domination. They certainly could not and did not claim a role in the unrealized dream of a reformed Bulgarian Church.

The Bulgarian perspective does not provide a more favorable conclusion regarding the effect of the American Board's presence in the region. While more or less recognizing missionary contributions, predominantly in the area of education as well as in literary life, both contemporary and present-day Bulgarians do not consider them essential or as pacesetting. Indeed, it would be difficult to find a single sphere of missionary involvement which had a decisive impact on the respective native development. Probably the only exception to this is in the area of the dissemination of information about the Bulgarians to English-speaking audiences. These propaganda functions, however, related both to American and to Bulgarian society. As suppliers of information, which was always colored by the missionary comprehension of things, the members of the European Turkey Mission might, indeed, claim an exclusive contribution to the molding of opinions among English-speakers.

In all other strictly Bulgarian historical developments, the missionaries had a much more modest effect. They fulfilled, at times, the role of a supplementary source of cultural emancipation among the natives but never became a predominant or model-setting source. In light of all assembled evidence, then, it would be appropriate to conclude that the missionaries of the American Board did much in Bulgaria but accomplished little.

* See page 76

List of References

1. James L. Barton, D. D. *Daybreak in Turkey*, 2nd ed., (Boston: The Pilgrim Press, 1908), p. 173.

2. Jean Haythorne Braden, "The Eagle and the Crescent: American Interests in the Ottoman Empire, 1861-1870," (Ph.D. dissertation, The Ohio State University, 1973), p. 76.

Bibliography

Primary Sources: Unpublished

Hilandar Research Library, The Ohio State University. Clarke Papers.

Hilandar Research Library, The Ohio State University. Haskell Papers.

Houghton Library, Harvard University. Papers of the American Board of Commissioners for Foreign Mission. 16.9, Vols. 4-20.

Primary Sources: Published

"The A. S. G. of Yesterday." *Samokov News* 1 (January 1923): 3-5.

Amerikanskata Kolegiia v gr. Samokov. Samokov, n.d.

Arnaudov, M., ed. *Arkhiv na G. S. Rakovski*. Vol. 1. Sofia, 1952.

Bagranoff, Tzvetko S. *The American Missions' Share in the Regeneration and Defense of Bulgaria*. American Bulgarian Good Neighbor League, 1947.

Barton, James L. *Daybreak in Turkey*. 2nd ed. Boston: The Pilgrim Press, 1908.

/Clarke, J. F./. "Mission Work among the Bulgarians." *The Bulgarians*. American Board of Commissioners for Foreign Missions, n.d.; reprint ed., *Missionary Herald* (June 1882).

Clarke, J. F. *Report of Relief Work for Bulgarian Refugees from Macedonia*. Samokov, 1904.

————. *Sketch of the European Turkey Mission of the American Board*. Boston: American Board of Commissioners for Foreign Missions, 1901.

————."Temperance Reform in Bulgaria." *The Union Signal* (Evanston, Ill.), November 30, 1911: 1-2.

————. *Temperance Work in Bulgaria*. Samokov, 1914.

Dinekov, Petŭr. *Sofiia prez XIX vek do Osvobozhdenieto na Bulgariia.* Sofia, 1937.

Dokumenti za bŭlgarskata istoriia. Vol. 1. Sofia, 1931. Vol. 2. Sofia, 1932.

Enicherev, Nikola Ganchev. *Vŭzpominaniia i belezhki.* Sofia, 1906.

Hamlin, Cyrus. *Among the Turks.* New York: Robert Carter and Brothers, 530 Broadway, 1878.

—————. "Bulgaria and Bulgarians." *The Missionary Review of the World.* Vol. 6. /New Series/, pp. 122-131.

—————. *My Life and Times.* 2nd ed. Boston and Chicago: Congregational Sunday School and Publishing Society, 1893.

Haskell, Edward B. *American Influence in Bulgaria.* New York, 1919; reprint ed., *The Missionary Review of the World* (January 1919).

—————. *Points Picked from the Annual Meeting of the European Turkey Mission, Samokov, Bulgaria Apr. 12-19, 1892.* Samokov, n.d.

House, J. H. "Village Life in Bulgaria." *The Bulgarians.* American Board of Commissioners for Foreign Missions, n.d.; reprint ed., *Missionary Herald* (October 1882).

Ikonomov, T. *Protestantskata propaganda u nas i neinite polzi za Bŭlgariia.* 3rd ed. Shumen, 1892.

Iliev, Atanas T. *Spomeni.* Sofia, 1926.

—————. *Urotsi ot Amerika po politichesko vŭzpitanie.* Stara Zagora, 1909.

Karavelov, Liuben. *Sŭbrani sŭchineniia.* Vol. 7. Sofia, 1967.

Madzharov, Mikhail. *Spomeni.* Sofia, 1925.

Marsh, George D. *Report of Relief Work in Adrianople Vilayet, 1904-1906.* Samokov, n.d.

Mishew, D. *America and Bulgaria and Their Moral Bonds.* Bern: Paul Haupt, Akademische Buchhandlung, 1918.

"Mission to European Turkey." *Missionary Herald* (December 1870): 387-390.

Ostrander, L. F., ed. *Fifty Years in Bulgaria*. Samokov, 1911.

Ostrander, L. F. *Amerikanskoto nauchno bogoslovsko zavedenie v Samokov*. Samokov, n.d.

Pears, Edwin, Sir. *Forty Years in Constantinople*. New York: Appleton and Company, 1916.

Report of the Central Committee for the Relief of Distress in Bulgaria and c.. Constantinople: A. N. Boyajian, 1877.

Riggs, Elias. *Reminiscences for My Children*. N.p., 1891.

/Rowland, Paul/. *The Samokov American Schools. Sixty Years of Service in Bulgaria*. Boston, 1924.

The Samokov Girls' School. Chicago: Woman's Board of Missions of the Interior, 1907.

"The School Choir." *Samokov News* 1 (May 1923): 3-4.

Schuyler, Eugene. *Selected Essays*. Memoir by Evelyn Schuyler Schaeffer. New York: Charles Scribner's Sons, 1901.

Shopov, A. *Bŭlgarii͡a v t͡surkovno otnoshenie*. Plovdiv, 1889.

The Thessalonica Agricultural and Industrial Institute for the Christian Industrial Training of Macedonian Boys. Annual Report, 1909. Thessalonica, 1910.

Thomson, Robert. "The Jubilee of Evangelical Work in European Turkey." *Missionary Herald*, November 1908, pp. 501-503.

T͡sanov, A. S. "D-r I. F. Klark." *Zornit͡sa* (Plovdiv), July 13, 1916, p. 2.

———. "Istorii͡ata na Bŭlgarskoto Evangelsko Blagotvoritelno D-vo." *I͡ubileina kniga na Bŭlgarskoto Evangelsko Blagotvoritelno Druzhestvo po sluchaĭ petdeset-godishninata mu 1875-1925*. Sofia, 1925, pp. 5-13.

Vagner, Ian. "Ot knigata 'Iz evropeiskii͡a Iztok. Ochert͡si ot pŭtuvanii͡ata mi iz Bŭlgarii͡a, Turt͡sii͡a, Germanii͡a i Rusii͡a'." Bŭchvarov, Ianko, ed. *Bulgarii͡a prez pogleda na cheshki pŭteshestvenit͡si*. Sofia, 1984, pp. 207-263.

Vatralski, Stoi͡an Krŭstev. *Amerika i Bŭlgarii͡a*. Sofia, 1933.

Washburn, George. *Fifty Years in Constantinople and Recollections of Robert College*. Boston and New York: Houghton Mifflin Company, 1909.

————. "Religious Liberty in Bulgaria." *The Independent* 35 (May 3, 1883): 2.

Primary Sources: Periodicals

Madedoniia͡ (Istanbul). 1867-1871.

Missionary News from Bulgaria. Nos. 1-55.

Turt͡siia͡ (Istanbul). 1866.

Zornit͡sa (Istanbul). 1864-1871, 1876-1896.

Zornit͡sa (Plovdiv). 1902-1911.

Secondary Sources

Anderson, Rufus. *History of the Missions of the American Board of Commissioners for Foreign Missions to the Oriental Churches*. 2 vols. Boston: Congregational Publishing Society, 1872.

Atanasov, Zhecho. *Istoriia͡ na bŭlgarskoto obrazovanie*. 2nd ed. Sofia, 1974.

Baldwin, Stephen L. *Foreign Missions of the Protestant Churches*. New York: Eaton and Mains Press, 1900.

Braden, Jean Haythorne. "The Eagle and the Crescent: American Interests in the Ottoman Empire, 1861-1870," Ph.D. dissertation. The Ohio State University, 1973.

Brailsford, H. N. *Macedonia. Its Races and their Future*. New York: Arno Press and the New York Times, 1971.

Carver, William Owen. *The Course of Christian Missions. A History and an Interpretation*. New York, Chicago, London and Edinburgh: Fleming H. Revell Company, n.d.

Clarke, James F. "Americans and the April Uprising." *East European Quarterly* 11/4 (Winter 1977): 421-428.

————. *Bible Societies. American Missionaries and the National Revival of Bulgaria*. New York: Arno Press and the New York Times, 1971.

————. "Protestantism and the Bulgarian Church Question in 1861." McKay, Donald C., ed. *Essays in the History of Modern Europe*. Freeport, New York: Books for Libraries Press, Inc., 1968.

———. "Reporting the Bulgarian Massacres: 'The Suffering in Bulgaria,' by Henry O. Dwight and the Rev. J. F. Clarke (1876)." *Southeastern Europe/L'Europe du Sud-Est* 4, part 2 (1977): 278-296.

Curti, Merle. *American Philanthropy Abroad: A History*. New Brunswick, New Jersey: Rutgers University Press, 1963.

Daniel, Robert L. *American Philanthropy in the Near East 1820-1960*. Athens: Ohio University Press, 1970.

DeNovo, John A. *American Interests and Policies in the Middle East 1900-1939*. Minneapolis: The University of Minnesota Press, 1963.

Dodge, Bayard. "American Educational and Missionary Efforts in the Nineteenth and Early Twentieth Centuries." *The Annals of the American Academy of Political and Social Science* 401 (May 1972): 15-22.

Dwight, Henry Otis, Tupper, H. Allen, Jr., and Bliss Edwin Munsell, eds. *The Encyclopedia of Missions*. 2nd ed. New York and London: Funk and Wagnalls Company, 1904.

Earle, Edward Mead. "American Missions in the Near East." *Foreign Affairs* 7/3 (April 1929): 398-417.

Field, Henry M. *The Greek Islands and Turkey after the War*. New York: Charles Scribner's Sons, 1902.

Field, James A., Jr. *America and the Mediterranean World 1776-1882*. Princeton, New Jersey: Princeton University Press, 1969.

———. "Trade, Skills, and Sympathy: The First Century and a Half of Commerce with the Near East." *The Annals of the American Academy of Political and Social Science* 401 (May 1972): 1-14.

Finnie, David H. *Pioneers East. The Early American Experience in the Middle East*. Cambridge, Massachusetts: Harvard University Press, 1967.

Genchev, Nikolai. *Bŭlgarsko Vŭzrazhdane*. Sofia, 1978.

Grabill, Joseph L. *Protestant Diplomacy and the Near East. Missionary Influence on American Policy, 1810-1927*. Minneapolis: University of Minnesota Press, 1971.

Griscom, Lloyd G. *Diplomatically Speaking*. New York: The Literary Guild of America, Inc., 1940.

Hall, William Webster, Jr. *Puritans in the Balkans. The American Board Mission in Bulgaria, 1878-1918. A Study in Purpose and Procedure*. Studia Historico-Philologica Serdicensia. Supplementi. Vol. 1. Sofia, 1938.

Iordanov, Vel. "Uchastieto na Amerika v nasheto vŭzrazhdane." *Uchilishten pregled* (Sofia) 35 (September 1936): 933-940.

Istorii͡a na obrazovanieto i pedagogicheskata misŭl v Bŭlgarii͡a. Vol. 1. Sofia, 1975.

Klark, Dzheims F. "Amerikant͡site otkrivat bulgarite: 1834-1871." *Bŭlgarii͡a v sveta ot drevnostta do nashi dni*. Vol. 1. Sofia, 1979, pp. 477-485.

Laurie, Thomas. *The Ely Volume: or, the Contributions of our Foreign Missions to Science and Human Well-Being*. 2nd ed., revised. Boston: American Board of Commissioners for Foreign Missions, Congregational House, 1885.

Mojzes, Paul Benjamin. "A History of the Congregational and Methodist Churches in Bulgaria and Yugoslavia." Ph.D. dissertation. Boston University, 1965.

Nachov, Nikola. "Novobŭlgarskata kniga i pechatnoto delo u nas ot 1806 do 1877 god." *Sbornik na Bŭlgarskata akademii͡a na naukite* 14: 1-132.

— — — —. *T͡sarigrad kato kulturen t͡sentŭr na bŭlgarite do 1877 godina*. Sofia, 1925.

Nikolov, Iordan. "Borbata na Matei Preobrazhenski protiv protestantskata propaganda." *Izvestii͡a na Instituta za istorii͡a* 18: 213-230.

— — — —. "Vasil Cholakov i protestantskata propaganda prez Vŭzrazhdaneto." *Istoricheski pregled* 4 (1969): 89-102.

Pantev, Andrei. "Bŭlgarskii͡at vŭpros v Anglii͡a i SASHT 1876-1903." Ph.D. dissertation. SU "Kliment Okhridski," 1984.

Pantev, Andrei, Petkov, Petko. *SASHT i Bŭlgarii͡a po vreme na Pŭrvata svetovna voina*. Sofia, 1983.

Shishmanov, Iv. D. "Novi danni za istoriiata na nasheto vŭzrazhdane." *Bŭlgarski pregled* 4 (February 1898): 53-78.

Shopov, Petur. "Pŭrvi ezikovi i kulturni vrŭzki mezhdu bŭlgari i severoamerikantsi." *Istoricheski pregled* 6 (1978): 78-83.

-----. "Propagandnata i prosvetna deinost na amerikanskite bibleiski obshtestva v bŭlgarskite zemi prez XIX v." *Izvestiia na Instituta za istoriia* 23: 149-184.

Stanimirov, Stanimir St. *Istoriia na Bŭlgarskata Tsŭrkva*. 3rd ed. Sofia, 1925.

Stavrianos, L. S. "The Influence of the West on the Balkans." Jelavich, Charles and Barbara, eds. *The Balkans in Transition. Essays on the Development of Balkan Life and Politics Since the Eighteenth Century*. Archon Books, 1974.

Stephanove, Constantine. *The Bulgarians and Anglo-Saxondom*. Berne: Paul Haupt, Librarie Academique, 1919.

Stoianov, Man'o. *Bŭlgarska vŭzrozhdenska knizhnina*. Vol. 1. Sofia, 1957.

-----. "Nachalo na protestantskata propaganda v Bulgariia." *Izvestiia na Instituta za istoriia* 14-15: 45-67.

-----. "Petko R. Slaveikov i protestantskata propaganda u nas." *Rodina* (Sofia) 3 (Marsh 1941): 90-98.

Strong, William E. *The Story of the American Board. An Account of the First Hundred Years of the American Board of Commissioners for Foreign Missions*. Boston, New York, Chicago: The Pilgrim Press, 1910.

Sugarev, Atanas. "Roliata na chitalishte 'Videlina' v obshtestveniia i kulturen zhivot na Panagiurishte." *Panagiurishte i Panagiursko v minaloto*. Sofia, 1956, pp. 269-286.

Todorov, Tzvetan. *The Conquest of America*. Translated by Richard Howard. New York: Harper and Row, Publishers, 1984.

Traikov, Veselin. "Protestantskite misioneri i borbata na bŭlgarskii͡a narod za t͡surkovna svoboda." *Bŭlgarii͡a v sveta ot drevnostta do nashi dni.* Vol. 1. Sofia, 1979, pp. 461-468.

T͡svetkov, Andrei. "G. S. Rakovski i bŭlgarskii͡at cherkoven vŭpros." *Georgi Stoikov Rakovski. Vŭzgledi, deinost i zhivot.* Vol. 1. Sofia, 1964, pp. 111-150.

Wiener, Leo. "America's Share in the Regeneration of Bulgaria (1840-1859)." *Modern Lanuage Notes* (Baltimore) 13 (1898): 65-81.

Index